What people are saying about …

THIS INVITATIONAL LIFE

"Steve Carter has been a close friend of ours for more than a decade, and the life he describes in this beautiful book is the life we've watched him lead day in and day out. Steve is one of the most genuinely curious people I know, and he's so incredibly passionate about loving people well, even—or especially—people who are different or forgotten or marginalized in some way. Steve lives this message better than anyone I know. He's been teaching me how to live this invitational life for years, and I'm so excited that through these pages, he can inspire you toward this way of living as well."

Shauna Niequist, author of *Bread & Wine* and *Savor*

"An invitation to join the greatest adventure of all time! Steve's words will challenge and motivate you to live a life that points others to the Author of life itself … Prepare to be inspired!"

Kirk Cousins, NFL quarterback for
the Washington Redskins

"Early on in this book, Steve Carter asks us a brilliant question: 'Who is welcome at your table?' He then goes on to remind us that the gospel of Jesus is a peace-making, bridge-building, and barrier-destroying way of life—where all are invited to the feast. He tells of a Savior whose arms of grace are open wide to all, and he encourages us to adopt the very same approach—welcoming even those we don't understand or those who are nothing like we are. Steve's excellent writing connects us with God's beating heart for all of humanity and teaches us the powerful principles of the invitational life."

Matt Redman, worship songwriter and recording
artist and author of *10,000 Reasons*

"Steve Carter has an infectious passion for helping people encounter Jesus Christ. As teaching pastor of one of the world's most dynamic and inspirational churches, he has lots of experience of living 'this invitational life.'"

Nicky Gumbel, pioneer of the Alpha Course
and vicar of Holy Trinity Brompton

"In a culture that is so divisive and polarizing, Steve Carter has written a beautiful and compelling book that captures the heart of God. *This Invitational Life* is a much-needed reminder that love is not nebulous or just theoretical. Love serves, washes feet, sacrifices, forgives, embraces the hurting, and welcomes all to the table."

Rev. Eugene Cho, senior pastor of Quest
Church and author of *Overrated*

"Steve Carter shares the impetus of his passion in these pages. Surprising, engaging, inspiring, and motivating! This book will help anyone get off the sidelines and into the risky, adventurous, and love-filled life of following Jesus. Read it and take up the invitation!"

Major Danielle Strickland, Social Justice
Secretary, The Salvation Army, USW

"The invitation starts now. Pastor Steve Carter reminds us about the power of living an invitational life—everything we do is infused with eternal importance. We're meant to risk the ocean, living as bold as lions by stepping out into all that God has called us to. Steve helps us understand how to say yes to this type of living and open ourselves to a front-row seat in seeing God change lives."

Levi Lusko, pastor of Fresh Life Church and author of *Through the Eyes of a Lion*

"I so badly want what Steve is inviting us into. I want my heart, priorities, and story aligned with the things that truly matter to Jesus. Steve's words set not only the vision for this happening but exactly how to do it each day. I highlighted and underlined things like crazy because I want the core truths inside this book to be my own heartbeat."

Mike Foster, People of the Second Chance

THIS
INVITATIONAL
LIFE

THIS INVITATIONAL LIFE

risking *yourself* to align with God's heartbeat for humanity

STEVE CARTER

David C Cook®
transforming lives together

THIS INVITATIONAL LIFE
Published by David C Cook
4050 Lee Vance View
Colorado Springs, CO 80918 U.S.A.

David C Cook U.K., Kingsway Communications
Eastbourne, East Sussex BN23 6NT, England

The graphic circle C logo is a registered trademark of David C Cook.

The website addresses recommended throughout this book are offered as a
resource to you. These websites are not intended in any way to be or imply an
endorsement on the part of David C Cook, nor do we vouch for their content.

Unless otherwise noted, all Scripture quotations are taken from the Holy Bible, NEW
INTERNATIONAL VERSION®, NIV®. Copyright © 1973, 2011 by Biblica,
Inc.® Used by permission. All rights reserved worldwide. NEW INTERNATIONAL
VERSION® and NIV® are registered trademarks of Biblica, Inc. Use of either
trademark for the offering of goods or services requires the prior written consent
of Biblica, Inc. Scripture quotations marked THE MESSAGE are taken from THE
MESSAGE. Copyright © by Eugene H. Peterson 1993, 2002. Used by permission of
Tyndale House Publishers, Inc.; NASB are taken from the New American Standard
Bible®, copyright © 1960, 1995 by The Lockman Foundation. Used by permission.
(www.Lockman.org); NLT are taken from the *Holy Bible*, New Living Translation,
copyright © 1996, 2007 by Tyndale House Foundation. Used by permission of
Tyndale House Publishers, Inc., Carol Stream, Illinois 60188. All rights reserved.

LCCN 2016936450
ISBN 978-0-7814-1397-8
eISBN 978-0-7814-1541-5

The Team: Alice Crider, Keith Wall, Nick Lee, Jennifer
Lonas, Helen Macdonald, Susan Murdock
Cover Design: Amy Konyndyk
Cover Photo: iStockphoto

Printed in the United States of America
First Edition 2016

1 2 3 4 5 6 7 8 9 10

052716

For Hal

CONTENTS

PART IV: RISK

FOREWORD

I've snuck into more places than I've been invited to. Like many people, when I was young, I got it into my head that I'd never be invited to many of the places I was most curious about visiting. I didn't let not having an invitation stop me, although perhaps I should have once or twice. My curiosity about what I might find inside overcame my fears about what might happen if I went. This has been a principle that has guided much of my faith too.

The Library of Congress in Washington, DC, is one of the most beautiful buildings in our capital. It's more than two centuries old and is, in fact, the oldest institution in our country. It has 883 miles of shelving, holds 33 million books, and has the largest collection of maps in the world. One time while I was in Washington, DC, I snuck in to see what was inside. It was late at night and a film crew was shooting a movie. One of the doors was ajar, so I went in. I remember spending most of my time that evening ducking behind desks and stacks of books and hoping not to get caught. Unfortunately, because the lights were off and I had spent most of my time hiding, while I was indeed inside the Library of Congress, I didn't actually get to see much of what was there.

Years later, I actually did get invited to a closed-door, invitation-only event inside the Library of Congress attended by just a few dozen people. I'm not really sure how I got on the list. My first guess was that they had confused me with someone else. When you spend most of your life feeling not invited and you finally get an invitation, you don't ask a lot of questions—you go. This time I was wearing a suit instead of blue jeans, and we held documents drafted by our Founding Fathers instead of flashlights.

Inside at the event, I stood where I had hidden before and saw for the first time things I hadn't noticed when I'd snuck in. This time, the lights were on. That helped. But there was something more going on inside of me that evening. I realized the biggest difference wasn't just that the lights in the building were on; it was as if a light came on inside of me. You see, this time I knew I had actually been invited. As a result, I felt free to talk to the people around me, to explore the books I'd been hiding behind, and to take in all of the beauty surrounding me. While I had indeed been inside this place before, I realized I hadn't fully experienced it yet. There's a big difference between the two.

Steve Carter is a humble and wise guide, and he has written a terrific book about living out your faith like you were invited—and about risking yourself to invite others. It's like he found the main electrical panel and turned on all the lights. Then he found an endless pile of tickets and started passing them out to everyone he meets because he wants everyone to know we're all invited too. He hasn't just compiled a lot of information about Jesus in these pages, because he knows most of us have all of the information we need. Instead, in these chapters he gently leads us room by room through the gospel promises God has whispered to us over the wide arc of time.

This book is an invitation to align yourself with God's heartbeat for humanity. To see and unleash the redemptive potential in the people around you. It's a reminder that Jesus has thrown wide open the doors for you and that we get the privilege to stand at the door and welcome others in—loved ones, neighbors, friends, and strangers. Everybody. In short, this book reminds us of the beauty and power of living like we were invited and what can happen in the lives of the people around us if we'll let them know they're invited too.

Bob Goff
Founder of Restore International
and author of Love Does

INTRODUCTION

When we launched Willow Creek Community Church more than forty years ago, local churches were, by and large, entrusting the fate of the people in their communities who were far from God to parachurch ministries such as the Billy Graham Evangelistic Association and Campus Crusade for Christ. The notion of an average local-church pastor attempting to strategize and mobilize his or her congregation for evangelistic effectiveness was a stretch, to put it mildly. Few were even attempting it.

But at Willow, we were so young and clueless that we actually tried to fire up our Christ followers to reach their friends through a seven-step strategy that eventually became known as the "Seeker Movement." This movement took off among local churches, and while widely misunderstood, it did in fact result in millions of people around the globe coming to faith in Christ. Yet it always had its critics—and a shelf life that even we at Willow understood was limited. In recent years, I have wondered, *What new movement will God use to draw people to himself?*

In the last decade, as I have engaged with pastors all across the world, I have noticed a marked decline in evangelistic energy in local churches that has caused me many a sleepless night. While I celebrate the rise in compassion and justice activities in churches and the unquestioned excitement around worship, aside from the Alpha Course I have not sensed many new conversations happening about spreading the good news to those who live unaware of it.

A few years ago, I invited a young communicator to join our Willow staff. I did not know at the time that in addition to Steve Carter's incredible teaching gift, he also has a deep longing to see those who are far from Christ become reconciled. He wakes up early every morning to ask God to help him function personally each day in a manner that would draw cynics and skeptics into playful conversations with him about the claims and promises of Christ. Far from a "hard sell" approach, Steve's sincere love for people and his infectious belief in the power of the gospel result in countless conversations that eventually inspire people to investigate Christianity on its own merits.

The first time he referred to his evangelistic approach in a sermon at Willow, I heard him casually call it "this invitational life." I loved the phrase and asked him to weave it into more of his sermons at our church—to show us how we, like him, could live more invitational lives.

After all these years of leading at Willow, I'm still a sucker for a changed life. Nothing moves me more deeply than watching God transform other human beings and seeing their lives and legacies be redeemed for all eternity. It never ceases to amaze me that God invites you and me to partner with him by extending ourselves toward those we love, so they might experience this kind of redemption. In *This Invitational Life*, Steve captures God's heart for every human being—and then shares insights from his own significant experience in living each day *invitationally*. His approach goes beyond a mere movement. It's a way of life. And I challenge you—align yourself with God's activity around you and sign on for the invitational life Steve describes. But be warned: when you open yourself up to others on behalf of the God who loves them, your life will never again be dull. You'll see him transform people as he uses you in some truly remarkable ways. And in the process, you, too, will be transformed. It's the natural by-product of living *This Invitational Life*.

Bill Hybels
Founder and senior pastor,
Willow Creek Community Church
Willow Creek Association

#WELCOME

Last year I got a call I never wanted to get.

My mentor Hal had been killed in a tragic motorcycle accident. He was only forty-seven years old. I could barely absorb the words as I tried to blink back the tears already forming. Everything fell silent, and life suddenly seemed to move in slow motion. As I hung up the phone, my ears rang with the words, "I'm so sorry, Steve."

What do you do when you lose someone profoundly influential and irreplaceable? I could not—and still cannot—imagine a world without Hal.

It turned out many felt the same way I did. In fact, more than fifteen hundred people came from all over the world to pay their respects at Hal's memorial service. As people took their seats, the band on stage began playing a medley of his favorite songs. Hal's childhood best friend then opened the service by saying, "Welcome. Welcome here today. Those words so quintessentially sum up Hal, don't they? 'Welcome' would be an appropriate hashtag for Hal's life. Each of you is here today because you were welcomed and embraced by Hal. That's just who he was."

As person after person shared memories and prayers on stage, I took in the magnitude of Hal's influence. One thing that stood out to me as I scanned the jam-packed room was the diversity of those who drove, flew, or made other arrangements to attend the service. Seated side by side were conservatives and progressives, atheists and agnostics, evangelicals and Mennonites, straight and gay people, unchurched and overchurched. The local Muslim imam was even in attendance, expressing his grief and gratitude for a man who had worked tirelessly to instill peace in the community.

Hal's recipe for success? *All were welcome at his table.*

Over years lived and meals shared, coffees sipped, concerts and sporting events attended, and humanitarian initiatives started, Hal recognized that *everywhere* was holy ground and that *every moment* was an opportunity for God to be on display.

Hal embodied this invitational life. He lived knowing God's great love for him and others. He showed up and let others see the difference God made in his life. He related to other people in such a way that they were drawn into relationship with him. He risked himself to align with God's heartbeat for humanity. He dared to share the invitation for others to know Jesus.

As I flew back home to Chicago, I wondered what kind of diversity will characterize my own funeral. Will the people I've impacted in life be a homogeneous display of those who looked, dressed, and voted like me? Will they believe the same things I did? Or will my life represent something much more aligned with the way of Jesus and his disciples?

What about you? How open is your life to people who are nothing like you? Who is welcome at your table?

LONGING TO BELONG

More than seven billion people inhabit the earth today.[1] Millions, if not billions, of them are lonely and longing to belong. They yearn for meaningful connection with others. They want to love and be loved, and they want their lives to matter. They long for an invitation to be part of something significant. They're joining clubs, gangs, cults, religions, and causes in order to be accepted somewhere.

My friend Joe had a difficult start to life. Whether it was his dad dying of alcoholism when Joe was two, his cousin overdosing on heroin, or his girlfriend being tragically murdered, the closest people in Joe's life were taken from him. In response to this pain, Joe worked to secure a place within a community that would never abandon him. Meanwhile, a deep seed of rage had taken root and began to influence his behavior. Joe took to life on the streets, running with a local Chicago gang. He had a shaved head and letters tattooed on his knuckles spelling out the words *love* and *hate*. What's more, he was willing to harm others, which led him to a rival gang's headquarters one night. As Joe and other gang members pulled up, shots began spilling out of the house. They returned fire and began running for their lives. As they ran, Joe felt a hand on his shoulder. In an instant he flipped the person over and began pistol-whipping the assailant. Tense, afraid, and overcome with rage, he kept pummeling the individual until he realized the "assailant" was his best friend's girlfriend.

As a result, Joe was sentenced to six years in prison for attempted murder and aggravated discharge of a firearm. Sitting in prison, Joe began wondering what had led him to this six-by-eight-foot cell. The answer was simple: a deep yearning to belong to something, a desire to be known, and a hunger for purpose. When Joe was released, a friend invited him to visit Willow Creek Community Church. Joe had kept God at a distance, but he agreed to go anyway. At that seventy-five-minute Sunday-morning gathering, Joe discovered what he had been searching for his whole life: grace, peace, love, purpose, and belonging.

I believe we all want to live lives of profound significance in God's kingdom. We want lives that are risky, brave, and open to engage with every tongue, tribe, and nation. We desire the kind of lives that say, "All are welcome at the table." But often something keeps us from putting ourselves out there so we can become fully alive in Christ. Something stops us from making a colossal impact for the kingdom. Sometimes we overlook the magnitude of our own salvation and forget how much we matter to God personally. Sometimes we worry about what people will think of us. We fear rejection and don't want to be the "obnoxious, judgmental Christians" everyone avoids. We get so concerned about our own social survival that we overlook the lost and lonely people around us. But what if we were all more like Hal?

RIOT INCITER

It was my first day at Grand Rapids Community College, and I didn't know a soul as I walked across the main quad. Hearing muffled shouts coming from a bullhorn, I turned a corner to see some guy with a massive sign emblazoned with the words "You're Going to Hell!" I stopped in my tracks, instantly entranced by his energy and rage. He was screaming at students passing by, telling them they were destined for hell because of their sins.

A young woman stood there crying as he laid into her, yelling about how sinful and evil she was. A film major at that time, I had no desire to be a pastor, preacher, or any sort of spiritual leader. But something about this scene—with the girl cowering and crying as religious venom spewed all over her—got to me. And I just snapped.

I bolted toward the guy, grabbed his sign and bullhorn, and ran. I sprinted! I threw the sign on the sidewalk, stepped up on a nearby picnic bench, and began speaking through the bullhorn. I had no plan and no sermon outline, but I was filled with holy indignation and a lot of adrenaline. I turned toward the girl and began telling her about God's love. "God *loves* you! You are good! You can be free and whole and right again!" Then all of a sudden, three police cars showed up with sirens blaring. Before I could hop off the bench, two burly cops pulled me down and said I was being arrested for inciting a riot.

I hope "riot inciter" is still on my record. I really do, because it's quite possibly the greatest label anyone has ever given me.

So what happened inside me to make me snap like that? When I saw that guy shaming and degrading everyone in the name of God, I felt a profound sense of conviction, because there were times in my life when I was the one judging, shaming, and assuming. I felt a resolve well up from within that declared, "I don't want to be like that." It made me curious about how we're supposed to point people toward grace, the Father's unconditional love, and the kingdom of God in an authentic, winsome way.

Flipping through the Scriptures, I searched for examples of how to do this. It led me straight to the way Jesus oriented his life. I found myself asking questions like these:

How did Jesus invite people into the story of God?
How did Jesus invite people into the kingdom?
How did the first followers of Jesus do this?
How did the disciples live?

Time and again I learned it was through relationships, authenticity, and a willingness to be uncomfortable and misunderstood for the sake of the good news. Jesus and his disciples lived this invitational life, and in doing so they changed the world.

Many of us use the term *spiritual gifts* when we talk about inviting others to hear the gospel. For many years I did too. "Well, you know, they've got the gift. I mean, they're pastors and missionaries, so this is part of their calling." Then one day as I studied the Scriptures, I realized it's actually *everyone's* responsibility, including mine, to live this invitational life. But I also began to see that beyond a responsibility, the first followers of Jesus believed it was a *privilege*. God entrusted his story to them so that the whole world might come to taste and see how good the Father truly is.

THE WHOLE CITY

Paul and Barnabas seemed to know it was their privilege to share the gospel. They were the most profound risk takers in the New Testament, willing to leave the comforts of their environment and be sent out in the power of the Holy Spirit, according to Acts 13.

When they reached a town called Pisidian Antioch, they attended a service at the local synagogue. As Paul and Barnabas were seated and the service began, they went through their usual liturgy and prepared to receive the message. The leader then looked at them and gave them an opportunity to share. When Paul was asked to teach, he stood up and began giving a history lesson, narrating the profound movements of God through ordinary people in the Old Testament. The people loved what he was sharing!

Then Paul said,

> We're here today bringing you good news: the Message that God promised the fathers [in the Old Testament] has come true for the children—for us! He raised Jesus.… I want you to know, my very dear friends, that it is on account of this resurrected Jesus that the forgiveness of your sins can be promised. He accomplishes, in those who believe, everything that the Law of Moses could never make good on. But everyone who believes in this raised-up Jesus is declared good and right and whole before God. (Acts 13:32–33, 38–39 THE MESSAGE).

People will strive, push, and buy to be considered good, right, and whole. Paul knew these people were working hard to earn their positions, and he delivered a message they'd never heard before. By simply believing in Christ—his death, burial, and resurrection—you can be made good, right, and whole.

When Paul finished, people were stunned. They'd never heard anything like this before. Many came up to ask questions, wanting more details and clarity. They begged Paul and Barnabas to come back and speak the following weekend. Paul and Barnabas agreed to stay in the city, and "on the next Sabbath almost the whole city gathered to hear the word of the Lord" (Acts 13:44). Almost the whole city!

Scholars believe the city of Pisidian Antioch at this time had a population of roughly 50,000 people. The Jewish synagogue included somewhere around 200 people, and in one week Paul and Barnabas rallied almost the entire city of Pisidian Antioch to come to church. Seriously? For 200 people to reach 50,000, that would mean each person dragged 250 people to church. Can you imagine you and 199 people in your church being so fired up to share the invitation with others that you reached almost the entire city?

Let's put this into sharper focus. The sixth largest city in the state of Michigan is Ann Arbor, or what I like to call "Ann Arbaugh" in honor of Jim Harbaugh, head football coach of my beloved University of Michigan Wolverines. In the fall, residents wake up early, put on maize-and-blue jerseys, and drive to campus to watch their Wolverines play football in the Big House—one of the most uniquely designed stadiums in the country. It is basically a gigantic bowl dug into the ground, with the seating just a few stories above ground.

On September 7, 2013, the Notre Dame Fighting Irish drove almost two hundred miles to lose to my Wolverines. This game broke every attendance record in college football history as 115,109 people packed into the Big House.[2] The total population of Ann Arbor at the time was nearly 117,000,[3] so essentially the stadium could seat every person who called the city home.

Back to Pisidian Antioch. When the people began to show up, it became apparent that the synagogue wouldn't accommodate them all. So, according to scholars, the gathering was moved to the largest venue in the city: the amphitheater. What compelled a small Jewish congregation to reach its entire city with the good news? These new believers' excitement wasn't about a person with spectacular preaching skills. It wasn't because of a great worship set. They weren't compelled to grab every person they could simply for the chance to hear a charismatic personality speak. They were radically compelled by Christ's love. They had heard the truth that they were good, right, and whole through Jesus, and this spurred an urgency to spread the invitation to everyone they could.

Can you imagine the excitement, the energy, and the wonder at how a small remnant of the city had now pushed the church fully into the public sector? This little group was suddenly thrust into conversations that people were wrestling with. This congregation had become relevant to its city. But not everyone was happy about all these invited strangers showing up. They interrupted the system; they messed up the seating charts and protocol. The Scriptures say, "When the Jews saw the crowds, they were filled with jealousy. They began to contradict what Paul was saying and heaped abuse on him" (Acts 13:45). I envision some of those religious leaders scoffing as new people filed in: "This isn't how we usually do things! Really, *that* person is coming? I can't believe he had the nerve to show his face here."

Imagine what it must have felt like to be one of the people showing up for the first time. Think of all the work, all the years, and all the choices that led to that moment when he or she bravely came to hear teaching about God. Now think about the role we play in either assisting the Spirit in drawing others toward the Father's love or repelling them from it through our lack of grace. When we encounter change or differences, how do we respond as Christians representing God?

The religious leaders couldn't celebrate the changes in their community, so they cursed in anger at every word Paul spoke. You can always tell when a desire for protocol has replaced a desire for God. It looks like an unwillingness to embrace growth and a resistance to change. But you can't stop good news! Paul and Barnabas were undaunted by the negative reaction and pressed on with the thousands of people who responded positively. As a result, the message of salvation "spread like wildfire all through the region" (Acts 13:49 THE MESSAGE). Paul and Barnabas offered a spark of hope, and it began to bring freedom and new life to the region.

WE NEED MORE STORIES LIKE THIS

It's not always easy to share our faith with others. Actually, it's not easy to gain the trust and respect so we can talk with people about faith in a way they'll respond to positively. The world we live in today is fast paced and impersonal. We get to peek into one another's lives from a safe distance as we scroll and click and "like" what's presented online.

We are busier than ever, more productive than ever, and more isolated and socially disconnected than ever. According to the Centers for Disease Control (CDC), nearly one in ten people in the United States were depressed in 2006.[4] Surveys have also shown an increase in social isolation, as well as a "significant decrease in social connections."[5] Is it any surprise that we're losing the art of relationship? It's a gift to be invited into the life of another person—invited to see the flaws and failures along with the joys and successes. The invitational life isn't just about finding ways to invite someone into your faith; it's also about discovering how you can be invited into the lives of those around you.

A friend of mine wrote a song that says, "I've been invited—I want to share the invitation."[6] I still remember hearing those words for the first time and feeling something shift in my spirit. I realized I had accepted the invitation into life with God but hadn't done anything to move beyond that. I'd been given the gift of grace, and I felt a renewed desire to share the invitation.

When you get the chance to partner with God in bringing others to him, you never forget it. It's easily one of the most thrilling, satisfying, and moving experiences of your life. I almost broke down crying when I saw my friend Joe, fresh out of prison, enter the baptism waters wearing a shirt with the word *Redeemed* handwritten on it. One of Joe's friends had offered up a spark to invite him to church, and he accepted. Then when Joe accepted the invitation to trust God with his life, another wildfire ignited in Joe's newly redeemed heart.

I'm praying for more Pisidian Antioch miracles to happen today. Wouldn't you love to see them? Wouldn't you love to play a part in them? I want each of us to experience the thrill of watching how God can use a single winsome invitation to save a life, redeem a story, transform a family, and change a destiny forever. I want this invitational life to become a common lifestyle for Christians everywhere, so that together we can impact the world and populate God's kingdom.

The fundamental progression of an invitational life—and the progression of this book—can be broken down into four movements or sections:

> 1. *Live.* Get swept up in God's great love and know
> your own relationship with him. This invitational
> life begins with going deep with Jesus.
> 2. *Show up.* Live a life that demands an explanation.
> Live openly and transparently before others, so they
> see a difference in you and wonder what you have.
> 3. *Relate.* Engage in other people's lives. Listen to
> them and relate to their stories. Become interesting
> to people by being interested in them.
> 4. *Risk.* Trust God by leaving the familiar and
> stepping into the unfamiliar; risk yourself to align
> with God's heartbeat for humanity. Make the
> difference you were created to make in the world.

As you read this book, be aware of how the Spirit may be nudging you, revealing perhaps where you currently are and where you could grow. God calls all of us believers to risk ourselves to align with his heartbeat for humanity. All of us fall somewhere on the spectrum between fear and courage, between playing it safe and taking a risk. Let's consider how to first become aware of the invitational opportunities all around us and then become fully engaged in this invitational way of living.

In the following chapters I'll unpack the principles of this invitational life even more, but this adventure begins with each of us first committing to be open to new perspectives, challenges, and ways of thinking. This process will demand that we focus on the faces and places that God is sending us to.

As you read, ask God to show you specific faces of people to pray for—people who need to hear the invitation to life with Jesus. Write down their names and commit to pray boldly for them every day. Ask God to show you places to go where he wants you to put this invitational life on display. Maybe it's your child's school, the gym, your workplace, or your favorite coffee shop. Write down those places and pray boldly for them each day. Look for opportunities to join God in bringing the miracle of Pisidian Antioch into your neighborhood, school, church, city, and throughout the entire world.

When you say yes to this invitational and intentional way of living, you're saying yes to a front-row seat to seeing lives restored as they are brought into relationship with God. As you learn to hear his voice guiding you throughout your day, your impact in our world will be unprecedented. And while you are watching this transformation happening in the lives of those you've been praying for, God will be busy transforming your life from the inside out. By choosing to live this invitational life, you'll discover a deeper intimacy with God and a profound dependency on him. Are you ready to begin?

PART I
LIVE

1
MY STORY, OUR STORY

Who are you and why are you here?

Does anything drive us more than our desire to answer these questions? They're compelling questions, and everywhere you turn, there are answers. Sort of.

Culture wants to tell us who we are. Society has an opinion too. Corporations would like to tell us why we're here. Brands are eager to fill us with answers about who we are. They say we aren't enough. We're lacking. We need this product, that experience, and these friends if we're going to really be someone. For some of us, our jobs determine who we are and why we exist. We're here to succeed, impress, and achieve. We're here to do better and acquire more stuff than everyone else. Other sources say we're here to have fun.

At the crux and core of our faith is a truth, a proclamation of good news that best informs us of who we are and why we're here. It begins in Genesis, the opening of the story of God. It starts with creation, when God established how everything would look, function, and interact. Genesis 1:1 tells us, "In the beginning God created the heavens and the earth." God was in the beginning. He was there from the start. Central to understanding the narrative of Scripture is to recognize this is God's story. The next verse says that "the earth was formless and empty" (v. 2). In Hebrew the phrase is *tohu va bohu*, which literally means "utter chaos." The earth was nothingness. It was barren, empty, and without form. Darkness hovered over the surface of the deep. The only glimmer of hope is that the Spirit of God was there hovering over the waters. That's when God said, "Let there be light" (v. 3). He looked into the chaos and called for order.

At the end of every day of creation, God reflected on the beautiful progression of his masterpiece and called it good. On day six came the pinnacle of his work. This is the point in God's story when he created humanity in his own image. Like an artist in a studio, he began to form a man out of the dust of the earth. He breathed life into this man, and he animated this man to become a living being. God himself bent over his creation and softly, like a beloved's whisper, pushed breath into Adam's lungs, making him alive. So there you have the answer to our first question: Who are you? You're a child of God, created in his image, breathed into life by God himself.

God not only spoke things and people into existence, but he also formed them with his hands. A world that was formless and empty, God now formed and filled with an abundance of good things. *Creation* was the first movement of God's story. He then created for this man a partner and placed them together in the garden, a place that was safe and peaceful and harmonious. But we all know the harmony of this existence didn't last long. The second major movement in God's story was the *fall*. In the garden was a serpent representing evil, hate, and deceit. This serpent didn't want good to exist. He wanted the world to go back to chaos and emptiness. So the serpent approached the woman and told her lies that seduced her into disobeying God's right order of things. The serpent went after harmony and trust, convincing her that God was holding out on her.

The serpent said to the woman, "God knows that when you eat from [this tree] your eyes will be opened, and you will [actually] be like God, knowing good and evil" (3:5). Seeing that the fruit looked delicious, and wanting the wisdom of God, she ate it (see v. 6). She then gave some fruit to her husband, who took it and ate it. Then everything began to change.

The intention, goodness, and peace of the relationship were now distorted and fractured. The man and woman knew it instantly. Their eyes were opened, and they realized they were naked. Suddenly there was something else—shame and anxiety. Adam and Eve knew that the goodness of God's creation had been massively damaged, and they had to cover it up. The shame they felt about the broken trust manifested in a deep sense of vulnerability; they were exposed and they knew it. They made coverings out of fig leaves and tried to conceal their secret. When they heard God "walking in the garden in the cool of the day," they hid (v. 8).

God did something in that moment. He asked a simple question: "Where are you? Where's the image I placed in you, the goodness I gave you? Where are you?" (see v. 9).

Then God did two more things. First he declared that he was going to take care of evil once and for all, and then he made clothes for Adam and Eve. He sacrificed an animal, a foreshadowing of redemption. God provided clothes to protect the good image he intended for the man and woman. God is all about relationship, and this was his way of inviting Adam and Eve back after they had separated themselves and hidden from him.

The fall initiated a pattern of living called *the struggle*, the third movement in the story of God. When a significant breach of trust occurs, it creates a domino effect of behaviors designed to protect the secret and keep the pain at bay. We see it right away in Genesis. There is brother killing brother. There are people trying to be God. There is a whole group of humanity rejecting God and blindly doing their own thing. Sounds a lot like today, doesn't it?

In response to this hopeless pattern, God created a redemptive plan that involved a group of people he collectively called Israel. This name literally means "to struggle with," and that's an accurate description of the legacy of this community. In fact, the majority of the Old Testament documents this group of people saying essentially, "We want to be God. We want to have a king. We want to do our own thing" (see Exod. 32; Judg. 21:25; 1 Sam. 8:1–9; and Ps. 81:11). The Israelites forgot who they were and whose they were. They had a major identity crisis that stretched across generations. They were enslaved. They came to power. They forced other people into slavery. They forgot about God. They didn't put him first. They found themselves in exile. More pain. More captivity. More silence.

CREATION, FALL, STRUGGLE

When Israel found itself under the authority of a new superpower in Rome, God sent his Son. John 1 says that "the Word," meaning Jesus, became flesh. He moved into the neighborhood. We saw his glory. When Jesus entered this broken and struggle-filled story,

MY STORY, OUR STORY

he showcased what it means to put God first. He put on display the character and demeanor of God, showing us what it looks like when the goodness of heaven comes to Earth. Jesus proclaimed the kingdom of God. He was willing to follow God no matter where God asked him to go, even to Golgotha, the place where he died on a cross for the brokenness and sins of humanity. He fulfilled the fourth movement in God's story, which is *redemption*.

These first Christ followers saw his life, death, and resurrection. Then they were invited to join with God in the fifth major movement—*restoration*. It is the movement to participate with God in making this world everything he intended it to be. These first followers were formless in so many ways but were now being formed more and more into the likeness of Christ. These first followers, who were empty in many ways, met Christ and were filled with the Holy Spirit. They were sent off to be messengers, ministers, ambassadors, and reconcilers.

Creation.

Fall.

Struggle.

Redemption.

Restoration.[1]

This is God's story. Yet the most amazing thing is that God's story is my story, and it's your story.

I was two years old the day my biological father walked into my room, kissed me on the forehead, walked out the door, and never came back. The dream that God had of a mom and a dad raising a child was fractured and broken. This "fall" changed the trajectory of my life. It created an identity struggle within me that caused me to hide. As a kid I often wondered about why my dad left me. I felt immense shame because I assumed it was my fault.

The fall in my story conveyed the message that I was responsible for my worth, and I grew up believing I had to be good enough and perform well enough to earn my place in someone's life. It initiated a pattern of living in which I was always striving to earn another's love, and this extended to my relationship with God. I didn't trust anyone. If my earthly father left me, what would stop my heavenly Father from doing the same?

In junior high two amazing guys mentored me and changed my life. They took me under their wings and introduced me to Jesus, although it was years before I realized it. They simply embraced me, related to me, made time for me, and showed me what grace looked like. Eventually I decided I wanted to live my life with this grace-filled Jesus as my savior, my guide, and my rock. So I was baptized, and God began the great work of healing my broken, fearful, and ashamed heart.

From that point on—and for the rest of my life—I've committed to sitting and talking with people about the power of the good news. My own story reflects creation, fall, struggle, redemption, and restoration.

The name *Jesus* means "God saves," and it's a powerful and appropriate reminder of the holy work he set into motion when he came to Earth to set us free. God is mighty to save, and we want to tell people this profound truth. But God also named his Son Immanuel, which means "God with us."

Some of us live with a mighty-to-save approach to relationships. We forget about time, conversation, and trust building and skip straight to the need for a savior. Sometimes we drop a Jesus bomb on people and then walk away. We don't want to be known. We don't want to be seen. We just want to drop some truth and say, "I'm done." But we can't really save people if we're never with them. We can't save a drowning person unless we jump in the water with him or her. And we can't speak into people's lives without first learning who they are and what motivates them.

Then there are some of us who love to be with people but never want to talk about Jesus being mighty to save. We're afraid that if we bring up Jesus in a conversation, people won't want to be around us. We don't want to be pushy. We don't want be rejected. We silence the story of redemption that God has written for us so we can avoid awkwardness or separation. But we're not really friends with someone if we're unable to talk about what matters most to us.

For many Christians, the Bible doesn't start in Genesis 1; it starts in Genesis 3 with the fall. When that happens, we are living without the goodness of our origin. Instead, we are living within the pain of our fall and struggle. From that broken perspective, we approach the people in our lives as threats to hide from, just as the first people did when God came looking for them. We build walls to keep people out, and we look for reasons to separate ourselves from those who are different.

Sharing our faith is about the power of bringing the two amazing names—Jesus and Immanuel—together. God saves *and* God with us. Every person was created in the image of God. That means whether someone is a follower of Jesus or not, that individual has something to teach me about God.

I learned the importance of being open to what others can teach me while working as a pastor in Fullerton, California. One afternoon

I walked by a house that had been converted into a coffee shop. As I walked in and struck up a conversation with the owners, I realized this coffeehouse had been started to help teenagers transitioning out of foster homes. These teens worked there to gain work experience, earn money, and learn leadership skills.

Within twenty minutes of meeting, the owners shared with me statistics for eighteen-year-olds transitioning out of foster care. Without a job or the opportunity to attend college, the majority of these teens will find themselves incarcerated or pregnant. I saw the heart of God on display as the owners talked about this café. I told them about the church I was helping to start and asked if we could partner together. Soon our church began holding prayer meetings, classes, and small groups in this little coffee shop with the owners, who were passionate about helping kids successfully move beyond foster care. Thankfully I was open to hearing about other people's experiences and receiving what they could teach me. Without that initial conversation, where connections were formed, we would've missed significant opportunities to minister to teens.

THE ART OF STORYTELLING

When we experience redemption in our stories, when we learn to trust God and let him into our fall and struggle, he begins to heal us and make us new again. He brings us back to the garden, before the fall, when things were good. He calls us good, he sees us as good, and he invites us to share his good news with others. So we must begin our relationships in Genesis 1, with trust, acceptance, and peace.

If we call ourselves reconcilers of God but don't engage the pain of other people's stories, we'll do nothing to nudge them toward redemption and restoration. We'll end up reinforcing the shame, the wounds, and the fall in their stories, and we'll enable them to continue in their struggle without hope for redemption. But a relationship that begins with trust is a safe place for us to open up and share about the fall and struggle in our lives. When people trust that you are for them and see the good in them, they can stop hiding and let you see their wounds and shame. I love sitting with people and simply asking, "Will you tell me your story? Will you tell me about your life?"

This is all about embodying the name of Immanuel—God with us. Sin is a signal that something inside is broken. It is an open wound, revealing a person in desperate need of a Healer. As we get to know others and they trust us with their stories, we start to see their behaviors as indicators of their struggles. We won't be tempted to judge or condemn them. We want to get beneath the surface of sin to discover why they are choosing to live as they do. When that happens, people feel as if an ambassador of the true, holy God has seen and known them. We're all in a constant struggle to live from a Genesis 1 perspective, believing and searching for the good rather than hanging on to the pain of Genesis 3.

Ruth Bell Graham's tombstone reads "End of Construction— Thank You for Your Patience." That's awesome. Billy Graham's wife joined with God in the restoration of all things for the majority of her life, and yet her humble heart recognized that we are all in process. We are all "under construction." Even as we heal and grow, we are also being used to bring restoration to this world.

If you're still wondering who you are and why you're here, consider this: You are a child of the living God, and you were created for relationship with God and others. You're here to make a difference. You're here to show others Jesus—God saves. And you're here to show people Immanuel—God with us.

The cross reminds us that Jesus was at his strongest while he was at his weakest. The cross is what happened the moment your struggle became your redemption. That is a powerful story to tell. People want to understand how God met you in your addiction, how he met you in your abandonment, how he met you in your pain, or how he met you in your sin. They want to know how God restored you and invited you to lead others to restoration.

God's story is my story is your story is every person's story. Aligning yourself with God's heartbeat for humanity means diving into all of it.

2
FROM SIMPLE TO SACRED

A few years ago, my friend Greg joined our church staff in Orange County, California, as an intern. One day he stopped by my office and said, "Hey, you're helping me learn how to preach. On the side I'm a personal trainer and would love to train you in conditioning and fitness. For free."

When someone offers to train you for free, who cares what's being implied about your weight. You take him up on his offer. So Greg told me to meet him at seven o'clock the next morning and wrote down the address. "Don't be late," he added. Little did I know that the kind church intern was a dictator in his nonchurch role.

The address led me to a parking garage, and as I pulled into it, I could hear the bass pumping. Music blasted as I got out of the car and walked through the doorway.

Greg approached me and screamed, *"Why are you here?"*

"'Cause you invited me?" I responded.

"Why are you here?" he shouted again.

"Why are you yelling at me?" I asked.

"If you can't tell me why you're here, you won't embrace the pain and suffering when it comes, and you'll just quit. So tell me, *why are you here?*"

"I don't know," I mumbled.

Starting to look impatient, Greg said, "Okay, shout out the first thing that comes to mind when I ask you the question. Here goes: *Why are you here?*"

So with all my inner might, I screamed, "I want to look like Ryan Gosling!"

Greg just looked at me and said, "Really? In all my years, that's the first time I've ever heard that."

I quickly learned from my training time with Greg that you never maximize your full potential until you learn how to embrace suffering. And suffer I did. I also have yet to attain my Gosling goal.

Of course, suffering in the gym is one thing, but suffering goes to a whole other level in the nitty-gritty, rough-and-tumble parts of life. Which leads me to this question: Have you ever had one of those moments when you realized your life was built on sand and not rock? Where do you go when the storm comes, when the crisis hits, when the chaos swirls? What is left of your character and beliefs when tragedy strikes and your world implodes? At the bedrock-foundation level, what is your life built on?

One of the purest ways to grow as a Christ follower is to learn the art of suffering well. Most of us diligently try to safeguard ourselves from experiencing pain and discomfort. And perhaps that's why we often shy away from sharing our faith. Putting ourselves out there seems too risky, too uncomfortable, and we forget how much we stand to gain.

PROKOPE OR PROSKOPE?

The apostle Paul was no stranger to suffering for the cause of Christ. He wrote to the church in Philippi while he was in chains to tell them that what had happened to him had actually advanced the gospel (see Phil. 1:12). Usually when a leader is apprehended and thrown behind bars, a movement comes to a screeching halt. People scatter, and it all comes to an end. This little upstart church in Philippi had heard the rumors of Paul's imprisonment, and the members were beginning to question if this whole Jesus thing was even worth it.

Paul said, "It has become clear throughout the whole palace guard and to everyone else that I am in chains for Christ" (v. 13). Apparently he had a perspective greater than his circumstances. He understood the art of suffering and believed it provided a platform to share his story. Some use such an opportunity to point people to the dreadfulness of their circumstances, while others point people to the greatness of their God.

The whole palace guard had taken notice. Paul maintained a steely conviction that gave him purpose while he was locked in prison. To make matters even more inspiring, Paul had the audacity to declare that the gospel was advancing within the prison walls. The Greek word for "advance" is a military term, *prokope*, which means "taking ground against an opposing force." In the face of opposition, Paul knew the gospel was still taking ground. The kingdom of God was being made known even in such adverse conditions.

I imagine every person in that little church in Philippi saying, "Paul, are you sure? How is that even possible? Rather than advancing, the gospel should be hindered." Paul used a play on words with *advance* and *hinder*. The Greek word for "hinder" is *proskope*, which means "a stumbling block or an obstacle." In the face of adversity, when circumstances are not in your favor, does good still advance, or is it prevented from moving forward? Does good *prokope* or does it *proskope*?

My stepdad had an axiom he repeated when I was growing up. For instance, he'd bring out these words of wisdom when my basketball team was losing at halftime or when I faced a daunting challenge. He would pull me aside, put both hands on my shoulders, and say, "Steve, it's not fair and it doesn't make sense, but you know what you need to do. Change adversity into opportunity."

Something about those four words inspire me to this day. They taught me from an early age to persevere. We all encounter circumstances that can potentially bind us in proverbial chains. What are the chains you're wrestling with right now? A bad health report? A recent job loss? A child making poor choices? A broken marriage? Maybe you're dealing with a crisis that no one seems to care about. You could be grieving the passing of a loved one. Maybe you live with uncontrollable anxiety about finances. Are your circumstances dictating how you act, think, and feel about Christ?

Sometimes when we're facing pain or devastation, we search for someone to blame. Often, that someone ends up being God. What we see in Paul's time of adversity is his trust that God was good all the time. His faith also declared that the circumstances he was in, which were intended for evil, could still produce good. Some in Philippi saw Paul's imprisonment as an opportunity to seize power. They spoke a safer message and tried to use Paul's circumstances as a means of currying the favor of the people inside this church. Paul's theology was battle tested, rock solid, and convincing because it was built on the cross, the true essence of chains and suffering.

I don't know what adverse conditions you're facing, but I encourage you to look for the opportunity in what adversity you are facing. We can't have discipleship without suffering. Chains fortify. Circumstances strengthen. Adversity becomes opportunity. Your life becomes a picture of the way of the cross.

STAGES OF DISCIPLESHIP

Discipleship progresses through three stages. It begins with the simple stage and then moves into struggle and then becomes sacred.

1. Simple—a theory yet to be proved. You consider a life with Jesus as a beautiful idea. It sounds good on paper but hasn't yet been tested. Will it work? Will it hold up? You've found the cross and believe in its redemption, but you haven't yet picked it up for yourself. You stand at a distance from the cross and overhear the conversations about the way of Jesus. You can recite certain phrases and verses, but you've yet to live them out.

When Apple introduced the iPod, they used the slogan "1,000 Songs in Your Pocket."[1] For the first time ever, you didn't have to purchase a whole music album; you were able to buy any song you wanted from the album. If you're in the simple stage of discipleship, you've chosen the way of iPod theology, in which you choose a few "pop" verses or ideas for your spiritual playlist, but you haven't heard the whole album. Then life gives you an unexpected punch in the face—an introduction to suffering. You don't realize it at the time, but this is an invitation to a beautiful struggle.

2. Struggle—a title fight of the will. Bumper-sticker theology and Christian clichés don't hold up to the sheer complexity of life. Strugglers find themselves in the refiner's fire. This is the soil for the best possible discipleship fruit, and yet it's also the place most Christians avoid at all cost. It's the invitation to go deeper with Jesus as you wrestle with doubts, emotions, and pressing questions. It's here you discover what God is made of and what faith in him looks like when it's tested. Here, you take up your cross and follow Jesus into the pain you're facing.

While the simple stage *talks* about discipleship being a good idea, the struggle stage is where discipleship moves from concept to practice. This is where you find your real life in Christ and where others see you wrestle with your faith. In this stage either you'll press in to know God more or you'll blame God and turn away from him.

If you press into God during this time, you'll find yourself getting up from the mat, overcoming that unexpected right hook life threw at you, and embracing a faith that has now become sacred.

3. Sacred—the place where faith has been tested and proved authentic. You've weathered the worst and come out on the other side. Your faith is no longer simple but sacred. Your language sounds the same. You use similar words when you talk about your faith, but there is a weight behind each sentence—it's not just theory and ideas now. You *know* that God is good. Your faith will relentlessly point people to the life, death, and resurrection of Christ. This kind of life will declare, "If Jesus experienced the cross, so will I. If Jesus experienced resurrection, so will I."

In the simple stage, we look at the chains of adversity and ulti-mately ask, "What did we do wrong?" In the struggle, we look at the chains and fight to understand why it's happening. When we reach the sacred stage, we find a purpose and declare allegiance to Christ fearlessly. This is the beginning of joy.

This invitational way of living allows others the chance to see the real you in real time during real struggles. This is where your life and your struggles will provide you a stage, your pain a platform, your mess a message, your peril a podium, your misery a microphone. Why? To point people to God.

Paul understood this. He saw iron shackles as an opportunity to tell a better story. Because of this perspective about his chains, Paul said, "Most of the brothers and sisters have become confident in the Lord and dare all the more to proclaim the gospel without fear" (Phil. 1:14).

So many of us live on the edge of *simple*, staring down *struggle* and wondering if it's even worth it. When we see people unveil their personal struggles while simultaneously taking another step toward the cross, it inspires us to follow. Many saw Paul rejoice over and over while he was in chains. It inspired a groundswell of confidence from deep within, giving the church courage to proclaim the gospel without fear.

My friend once sat with a recovering addict. He had been sober for more than twenty years, yet he still made his way to recovery meetings five times a week. When my friend asked why he continued to go, the man quickly responded, "Every day, a new kid shows up, only a few hours sober and looking for a fresh start, and I know *if he makes it, I make it.*"

Paul refused to allow the chains, the adversity, the circumstances he found himself in to have the last word or dictate anything about his identity in Christ. The chains were an opportunity to go deeper with Jesus and invite others to dare to do the same.

Why are you here? If you hesitate to answer that question, it might be a clue as to where God is inviting you to grow. Perhaps you're living in the simple stage. You believe in Jesus but just want to have a nice, easy, low-key life, never risking your comfort to face the pain of rejection or disappointment. The problem is, if you stay there, you'll never really get to answer the question of why you're here, because it's only in the struggle that you catch a glimpse of why you're here. And without an understanding of why you're here, you can't get to that sacred place of authentic life with God.

It's in the sacred stage that we become effective at spreading the gospel to the ends of the earth. It's here we become a light in the darkness and a powerful invitation to others. In the sacred stage, we know beyond all doubt that if God is for us, nothing can ultimately be against us (see Rom. 8:31).

Authentic life with God is where we find joy and fulfillment and a deep sense of purpose. It's where the good work of Jesus gets done. Why are you here? I'm not sure about you, but to me that *sacred* life sounds like the best place to live.

3
BARRIERS OR CARRIERS

Remember as a kid the first time you felt left out? Everyone else got picked for kickball, and you were left standing there. My son told me the other night that his friends were talking about an upcoming birthday party, and he realized he didn't get invited. It crushed him that his "friend" didn't include him. He said, "I thought we were friends! Why wouldn't he invite me? Did I do something wrong to him, Dad? Is there something wrong with me?" This was the first time he experienced the pain of being left out. It's one thing when a second grader doesn't give you an invitation, but it's another when you are left wondering if God would ever welcome you.

When we peruse the pages of the Hebrew Scriptures, we see the invitation for the people of Israel to be a light to the nations. God invited them "to act justly and to love mercy and to walk humbly" with him (Mic. 6:8). The Hebrew people neglected to see the story God was writing and instead focused on the differences and subtleties that make human beings who we are. Out of fear of being negatively influenced by the culture, they began to use God's instruction to remain holy, not as a way to grow closer to God and others, but as a way to justify segregation. The Scriptures became a measuring stick they used to identify who was in and who was out.

These barriers created a polarization, segregation, and division that ultimately kept everyone in chaos and far from God's intended plan of oneness.

ANCIENT BARRIERS AND MODERN CARRIERS

When you entered Herod's temple, there were signs posted to keep people in their right places. In the past one hundred years, two of these warning signs posted at Herod's temple have been discovered. Translated, they read:

NO FOREIGNER
IS TO GO BEYOND THE BALUSTRADE
AND THE PLAZA OF THE TEMPLE ZONE.
WHOEVER IS CAUGHT DOING SO
WILL HAVE HIMSELF TO BLAME
FOR HIS DEATH
WHICH WILL FOLLOW.

Only those with the right lineage were granted greater admittance to the temple, and everyone else had partial access at best. They were relegated to an area with the rest of the Gentiles. The Gentiles were those people—outsiders—nobody wanted to be around. It didn't matter the distance worshippers traveled to come to the temple; they still could get only as close to God as their pedigrees allowed.

One day the apostle Paul showed up at the temple in Jerusalem to pray, make an offering, and conclude a purification process. He'd traveled with some friends who happened to be Gentiles, but he knew he couldn't take them with him deep into the heart of the temple. So they waited outside for Paul to return, eager to hear about his experience. As Paul walked toward the altar, some Jews from Ephesus and Asia saw him and began rioting.

They seized him and started screaming, "Fellow Israelites, help us! This is the man who teaches everyone everywhere against our people and our law and this place [the temple]. And besides, he has brought Greeks into the temple and defiled this holy place" (Acts 21:28). As a result, "the whole city was aroused, and the people came running from all directions. Seizing Paul, they dragged him from the temple, and immediately the gates were shut" (v. 30).

Paul was dragged out of the temple, and the religious leaders immediately shut the gates to God's house. These religious elitists disrupted everyone's prayers to stir up trouble, calling out threat after threat against Paul. Then they raised the bar by spreading lies that he snuck a Gentile into the temple, making everyone there unclean. Pandemonium ensued, and Roman troops came to arrest Paul.

In the 1940s, six million of our Hebrew brothers and sisters were executed for being Jews. In the fifties and sixties, racial tensions prevented African Americans from receiving Communion in some churches in the United States. In the 1990s, missionaries came home from Rwanda celebrating that 90 percent of the country had been reached for Christ. After which, genocide broke out, lasting one hundred days and costing an estimated one million people their lives.[1] The missionaries realized that the Rwandans' allegiance was first to their tribes and then to Christ. In 2014, there were roughly sixty million displaced peoples on the planet.[2]

This isn't an ancient issue—it isn't something that *happened*—it's something that is *happening*.

The world is not what God intended it to be. We only have to look at our news headlines to see the obvious separation that leads to death and destruction every day.

Paul saw the plight of his Gentile friends and how they were unable to access the fullness of God before Christ. He saw how the divide was growing between Jews and Gentiles—not just in the world but also in the church. In light of this background, Paul penned these words:

> Now in Christ Jesus you [Gentiles] who once were far away [from God] have been brought near by the blood of Christ.
>
> For he himself is our peace, who has made the two groups one and has destroyed the barrier, the dividing wall of hostility, by setting aside in his flesh the law with its commands and regulations. His purpose was to create in himself one new humanity [an entirely new race] out of the two, thus making peace, and in one body to reconcile both of them to God through the cross, by which he put to death their hostility. He came and preached peace to you

who were far away and peace to those who were
near. For through him we both have access to the
Father by one Spirit. (Eph. 2:13–18)

Paul was saying that Jesus is our vision for how we must orient our lives. In every relationship, we as Christ followers must
strive to see humanity through the kingdom lens. Our world
wants us to isolate and segregate, but when Jesus himself is our
foundation and framework, we experience a uniting gospel that
promotes oneness.

Is Jesus your vision for how you connect with others?
Remember when you stood on the outside, unsure if the God
of all creation would fully welcome you in? You had drifted far
from God's desire for your life. You became aware of it, and this
ache overwhelmed you. The gift of grace decimated your sin and
shame. It was here you found yourself welcomed into God's family with full access to the Father—all because of the cross.

The cross is a barrier killer. It's a bridge maker that invites us
into a new way of living. If there are people who have hurt you, go
to the cross. If there are people you hate, go to the cross. If you've
been betrayed, go to the cross. If there are people who irritate
you, go to the cross. Jesus himself is our peace, and through the
cross he came to make peace on the earth. Now it's our job—and
our privilege—to be peacemakers too. When we go to the cross,
and when we lead others to it, those barriers crumble and peace
reigns. We as Christ followers have the key to world peace, if and
when we take on this invitational life and lead others straight to
the cross.

When I talk about those people we push away or separate from, I'm not talking about people who are dangerous or abusive. There are circumstances where it's appropriate and healthy to break off relationships or distance ourselves from them. What I'm talking about here are the people who don't vote like us, think like us, live like us, or believe like us. These are people we can't stand or maybe just don't understand.

The cross obliterated the dividing wall and any form of hostility. It is in the process of making us into a new humanity, an entirely new race, a people who embody what the cross looks like in flesh and sweat and blood. Jesus made peace through the cross. He preached peace. All for what? So we could have full access to the Father. So that *all* could have access to the Father.

One meaning of the word *access* in Greek is "having an audience with the king." Jesus came so we can all have access to the King, including those who are different from us. At any moment throughout the day, you have an audience with God. You can sit in his presence, interacting with the designer and curator of all things. Allow him to father you through a difficult situation or remind you of his love for you.

One of the greatest gifts we have as followers of Jesus is to know deep within our core that God is with us and for us. Which makes me wonder: What walls have I erected in my life that prevent people from seeking full access to God? What are the barriers in your life?

Paul later said that our bodies are "temples of the Holy Spirit" (1 Cor. 6:19). So instead of going to a temple to experience God, people can now experience the grace and character of God through us. We are either living barriers or carriers of the gospel of peace, inviting people to fully access God through Christ. The result of reconciliation is access to the newfound privilege of entering holy ground. Paul put it this way:

> You are no longer foreigners and strangers, but fellow citizens with God's people and also members of his household, built on the foundation of the apostles and prophets, with Christ Jesus himself as the chief cornerstone. In him the whole building is joined together and rises to become a holy temple in the Lord. And in him you too are being built together to become a dwelling in which God lives by his Spirit. (Eph. 2:19–22)

Every person you know is just one prayer away from joining God's radically all-inclusive community that enjoys fellowship with the Father, Son, and Spirit.

The worst alcoholic you know *is just one prayer away*.

The angriest person you know *is just one prayer away*.

The biggest control freak in your community *is just one prayer away*.

The most dangerous criminal in your city *is just one prayer away*.

The most drug-addicted person you know *is just one prayer away*.

The worst terrorist in the world *is just one prayer away*.

The meanest boss you've ever had *is just one prayer away*.

The most narcissistic person you know *is just one prayer away*.

The most racist person you know *is just one prayer away*.

The most dysfunctional person in your family *is just one prayer away*.

The most hate-filled person you know *is just one prayer away*.

The most treacherous, evil, broken, despised sinner you know is *still* just one prayer away.

At one time *you* were just one prayer away. Do you remember the day you prayed that prayer? Do you remember how that one prayer changed everything for you?

BARRIERS VERSUS BRIDGES

Think for a moment about specific ways your life changed when you first accepted God's invitation into life with him. How did your relationships change? Did you find yourself with a newfound desire for reconciliation and forgiveness? Maybe you noticed hurting people sitting on the subway or passing you on the street, and your heart went out to them in a way it hadn't before. How did your self-worth change? Did you begin to believe that you have value and are deserving of love? Perhaps you made some personal changes—quit spending as much or walked away from an unhealthy relationship. Maybe shame lost some of its power in your life. When we choose to let God love us, it changes everything. When grace becomes true for us, the natural result is to view ourselves and others as precious and important.

Either our lives will be pictures of the cross, radically welcoming people to full access to God, or they will resemble Herod's temple, radically excluding people with barriers and segregation.

The cross welcomes.

Herod's temple excludes.

The cross goes deep and wide.

Herod's temple is shallow and narrow.

The heart of the cross is to draw the far near.

The heart of Herod's temple is to keep the far away.

Does your life represent the cross? Is it filled with a diverse range of people all over the spiritual spectrum? Is there always a seat open at your table? As Christ followers, we get to be inclusive of humanity, knowing full well we're all just one prayer away.

So how do we do it? It begins with Jesus. He is the full picture of what God intends our lives to resemble. He is our vision. He is our example of how to truly thrive. Think for a moment. Does a name come to mind as you're reading this? Pay attention to the Spirit and ask God to reveal any barriers in your life.

Jesus not only is our peace, but he also came to make peace. As his followers, we're to be the peacemakers. As Mother Teresa once said, "If we have no peace, it is because we have forgotten that we belong to each other." Have you forgotten? You belong to the person who irritates you, the one who hurt you, the one who is different from you. You belong to the people around you. This is why Christ came to make peace.

It's easy to have a one-sided faith. It's also easy to live safe and riskless lives in which we choose who we'll let in. But the truth is, we belong to each other. As difficult as it is, our calling is to offer an invitation, extending a hand of peace to both sides of the conflict.

A friend of mine struggled for years in his relationship with a sibling. As kids they were always put in situations where they had to compete for their parents' approval. Instead of seeing the similarities, these brothers saw their differences—and saw each other as an enemy. One day after a service, this friend walked forward and said, "I can't stand my brother, and I can't stand my parents for making me hate him."

After talking for a while, I asked my friend to read and reread Ephesians 2 several times. I then asked him to pray for God to soften his heart toward his family members. For weeks, first thing in the morning, he would read Ephesians 2 and kneel to pray.

Each weekend I would ask, "How's your heart toward your brother and your parents?"

His response was usually, "Not good. Not good at all."

Several weeks later when I asked him again, he said, "The walls are falling, and I'm beginning to catch a glimpse of how much God loves them."

Scripture and the Holy Spirit were changing him and helping him see the power of unity and the poison of disunity. He recognized the need for belonging and the need to end separation.

When we realize we belong to each other, our posture changes, we listen better, and we see others as God sees them. We see the cross in deeper ways. *You* are the closest that some people will ever get to a Bible or a church. Will your presence invite them to feel intrigued by the way you love them and see them? Or do your attitude and demeanor suggest that they only get partial access to God's love?

Jesus boldly proclaimed with his life that each and every person who walks this planet is always just one prayer away. Who in your life are you praying will find God?

We thrive when we allow the cross to decimate the barriers we have put up and exchange those barriers for a lifetime of being carriers of God's good news.

PART II
SHOW UP

4
BONE MARROW

My name wasn't always Steve Carter. When I came into this world, the name on my birth certificate read "Stephen Charles Born." Charles was my biological father's name, though everyone called him Chuck. I don't remember or really know much about Chuck beyond a few pictures that could easily have earned him a spot in the Mustache Hall of Fame. We lived in an apartment in Los Angeles, where my mom and dad managed the complex and dealt with the tenants. When Chuck left, the property-management company could easily have thrown us into the streets. But instead, they told my mom that if she'd take care of collecting everyone's rent, they would send someone to handle maintenance and repairs.

The man the property-management firm sent would often stop by our apartment and play Matchbox cars with me. His name was Joel, and he had a glorious full beard that would make any hipster burn with envy. Joel would get down on the floor and build race-tracks with me. We'd race cars for hours, laughing every time there was a big wreck. A few years later, my mom married Joel, and I started referring to him as my "new dad."

I discovered what it meant to be given a fresh start with a new identity. At this critical time in my life, I was in a sense "adopted" by a new father. This change sent my life in a new direction.

What I experienced physically, followers of Christ experience spiritually. We are adopted by a loving Father and given a new identity. The change sends our lives in a new direction. It turns out that the apostle Paul had important things to say about this concept, especially when he wrote a letter to the emerging church in Ephesus.

NO STRINGS ATTACHED

In the first century, Ephesus was the second-largest city in the world, with a quarter-million people calling it home. Greek and Roman cultures greatly influenced this sophisticated city. Ephesus had an amphitheater overlooking the city, with a capacity to hold twenty-five thousand people.

As Alexander the Great began conquering the world, his desire was always for "the Greek Way," also known as Hellenism, to spread around the world. So people would sit watching a play with the gymnasium, library, schools, courtyards, and the agora (a huge gathering place) in the background. Ephesus was home to the temple of Artemis, which historians have named one of the Seven Wonders of the World.

It was good to live in Ephesus, and Alexander didn't want anyone to forget it. In the ancient Near East, this was how authorities and the "chamber of commerce" would market their cities—with buildings, sculptures, drama, commercial centers, and a vibrant cultural scene. This is the context in which the apostle Paul wrote a letter to an upstart church reminding its members that amid this affluence and power, Christians were to stay rooted and established in the things that mattered to God.

If Paul were writing epistles today, he would probably remind us of the same thing. After all, corporations spend hundreds of billions of dollars a year in the United States on online and television marketing. Their strategies consistently overpromise and underdeliver, telling us how to achieve wealth, popularity, status, and sex appeal. They assure you that buying their products or following their programs will create an identity that will make everyone else want to be you. Those billions of dollars are spent to shape what you believe or long to be true about yourself. Can you notice ways this strategy is in fact working? After watching a certain ad, do you find yourself feeling inferior? Are you aware of an increased desire to stand out after spending time on certain websites?

Today's marketing and advertising might be more sophisticated and widespread than in earlier times, but the pressures to impress and "be someone" seem to be common to humans no matter the era. For instance, Greek culture was obsessed with the human body. They worshipped the physical form. The great artists of the day exalted the body through sculpture. Everyone could walk the main streets and see sculptures highlighting the ideal body. To these artists, the perfect physique was that of an athlete—muscular, fit, and imposing.

Ancient Greeks believed that their gods took on human form, and to properly worship them, people adorned their temples with life-size, lifelike images of these gods. If temples were filled with sculptures of athletic, strong, toned gods, what do you think was being culturally implied? "You better look like this. That ideal is what you should be striving for." Sound familiar?

If you've ever stood in the checkout line at your local grocery store and scanned the magazine rack, you've probably felt the pressure. The message is "Aim for perfection if you want to be accepted." In Ephesus during Paul's time, there was an underlying pressure to do whatever it took to look perfect. If a culture is built on a certain ideal, what happens when that ideal isn't achieved? In Greek culture, if people's bodies didn't meet the ideal, they were pushed to the fringes of society. Not only would they be excluded, but their lack of discipline to be godlike would also put a strain on the entire family. Anything less than perfect, healthy, and desirable was considered failure.

In Ephesus, laws were enacted to remove imperfection. One of the most tragic examples of this was a legal practice called *exposi*, which was the practice of exposing infants. Any child who was deformed, disfigured, handicapped, or simply unwanted could be taken outside the city and left to die. If a woman struggled to get pregnant in those days, she could walk up the mountain and pick through the bodies to find a living child to take as her own. Roman law recognized that if any child was left there intentionally, you could take it as your own.

As if that wasn't tragic enough, bottom-feeders, such as sex traffickers and brothel owners, frequented the place of disposal, viewing it as a convenient and cheap way to raise the next generation of slaves. Why buy a slave when you could just raise one? In fact, Ephesus was the slave capital of the first century. One of the underlying spiritual strongholds of this culture was that anything seen as deformed, defective, or unwanted should be discarded.

In the middle of all this, a church was started and became the hope of Ephesus. What do you imagine was the demographic of the church? Young. Old. Single. Married. Masters. Slaves. In light of this background, consider how Paul described what God believed to be true about each and every person in Ephesus:

> [God] chose us in him [Christ] before the cre-
> ation of the world to be holy and blameless in his
> sight. In love he predestined us for adoption to
> sonship through Jesus Christ, in accordance with
> his pleasure and will—to the praise of his glorious
> grace, which he has freely given us in the One
> he loves. In him we have redemption through his
> blood, the forgiveness of sins, in accordance with
> the riches of God's grace that he lavished on us.
> (Eph. 1:4–8)

To a city intent on attaining physical perfection, Paul pro-claimed, "In love, God chose you—no strings attached."

No one is perfect. Those who appear perfect have just mastered the art of using smoke and mirrors, because it's all an illusion. Trying to maintain a degree of impossible perfection all day, every day must have been exhausting for the Ephesians. But what if your "flaws" could not be hidden? What if your only understanding of God was something completely unattainable to you? What if you grew up in a society that pushed you aside and allowed for a belief system that encouraged your parents to abandon you? Your view of God would be extremely messed up.

Can you imagine what it must have been like to hear Paul say that God chose you? In love, God adopted you. The Greek gods neglected you, but the God of all creation pursued and adopted you. *Adoption* was a word everyone understood in that day. The process of adoption required that it be public. The father chose the child, the child had to willingly accept, any past debts would be canceled, and the child would be given a new identity.

Adoption made a way when it looked as if all was lost. For those who don't meet the social expectation of what it looks like to fit in—outcasts, oddballs, and iconoclasts—do we understand what Paul was saying here? Let it sink in that there is a place for you in God's family.

When my mom remarried, Joel agreed to accept me as his son. So my biological father signed away all his rights, and a process began for Joel to adopt me. I met with a judge in Malibu, California, and was asked a plethora of questions about my "new dad." I was given the chance to receive a new middle and last name. My mom told me I could choose any name I wanted, which was pretty cool for a four-year-old.

I didn't tell anyone my choice beforehand, so when the judge asked my preferred middle name, I declared, "I want my name to be Stephen Poncherello Carter." This was after Erik Estrada's character from my favorite TV show *CHiPs*.

My mom quickly replied, "Nope! No way. It will be Ryan. You don't want a name that's going to get you beat up in junior high."

So I left the courthouse with a new birth certificate, an acceptable middle name, a new last name, and a new dad.

Have you ever felt abandoned? Neglected? Discarded? Have you received the message that you don't measure up? That you're unwanted? Have you ever longed for someone to show up to see you, know you, and say you're okay?

Paul painted a picture of God's character to the people of Ephesus in his letter. He affirmed that the cross is proof that God showed up and is running after you. This is the one true God, the one who runs up the hill and wraps you in his arms and declares that you are worth loving. You are good and valuable and have a beautiful purpose on this planet. This God sets you apart. This God makes you blameless in his sight. This God in his great love adopted you into his family.

At bedtime for many years to come after that court date, my new dad would tuck me in and tell me, "All the other parents were given children, but I actually got to choose—and I chose you."

The cross is God's declaration that "I choose you. Even if you were the only child on Earth, I would run up that hill and find you. You are mine." God didn't leave us exposed to the elements of sin; he didn't leave us to figure it out on our own, vulnerable to evil. His death canceled all of our debts and gave us a new identity. The cross for me is a profound adoption story where God says, "I chose you. I love you. Now will you be mine?"

I often wonder what my life would have been like if Joel hadn't shown up at that apartment complex. And I often wonder what my life would have been like if I had never experienced God showing up for me.[1]

A SECOND CHANCE AT LIFE

A few years ago, my dad constantly felt fatigued and thought he might have mono. So he went to see his doctor, who ordered blood tests and called him the following day. My dad's white-blood cell count was six times higher than normal, and he needed to be rushed to the hospital. Within a few days, he was diagnosed with acute myelogenous leukemia, an aggressive and deadly form of cancer, especially for someone my father's age.

Over the next four months, doctors in Grand Rapids, Michigan, began attacking the cancer with strong doses of chemotherapy. My dad had always been a resilient guy, but the chemo truly did a number on his body. Incredibly, after months of treatment he went into remission, and we all celebrated. The doctors said they would monitor him, and if he was cancer-free after five years, we would again be able to celebrate because he would be deemed cured.

Less than a week later, a phone call from the doctor's office brought us once again to our knees. The leukemia had returned more powerfully than before. Now the only medical option for survival was a bone-marrow transplant. The medical team did a rigorous search to find someone who was a complete, 100 percent match. Being adopted, I knew I wouldn't be a match. No one in his family was a suitable match, and out of ten million registrants—six million domestically and four million internationally—only one person was in a position to save my father's life.

The apostle Paul said, "I know what it is to be in need" (Phil. 4:12). Do you know what it means to be in need? Perhaps an experience you've had comes to mind? Perhaps you're in the midst of great need right now. Maybe you know exactly what Paul meant. You need a miracle. Underneath the need, you must surrender the outcome. You stand face to face with the illusion of control and can only ask and pray for help.

Only one person out of ten million was in a position to save my father's life. All we knew was that she was in her early thirties and didn't reside in the United States. To protect the privacy of the potential donor, the doctors didn't allow us to contact her. Which is probably a pretty good thing, because I would have stalked her, called her, and begged her. I would have done whatever I could to convince her to show up and save my dad.

We could only sit back and wait. We simply had to embrace our need. Our family spent most of the next few days on our knees in prayer as we waited for the donor's decision. When my dad's body was at its weakest, his faith became its strongest. His faith became so deep and so real. Sure, he wanted to live to see his first grandson—with whom my wife was pregnant at the time—but he would say things like, "Steve, when I said yes to following Jesus, I wasn't promised better health. I was promised forgiveness and the truth that God will always be with me and for me."

I was in awe of his contentment. It was as if he had discovered the secret Paul talked about. He was at peace. We waited a few days for the potential donor to decide. The process involved in collecting bone marrow is very painful and inconvenient. There are two ways: either you have the marrow surgically removed from your hip bones while you're under anesthesia, or you receive a week of medical injections that painfully force your stem cells to leave your bone marrow and transfer into the bloodstream before you undergo a six-hour blood donation. Neither option sounds appealing in the least, especially if you don't even know the recipient.

In an act of sheer grace, this woman we had never met chose to show up and give a piece of herself—a gift my father so desperately needed to live. Though we never met her in person, her selfless and courageous act saved my dad's life.

A few months after his recovery, my father wrote these words to his mystery donor:

> *I have a son whom I adopted when he was four years old. I have no natural children of my own. Early in our marriage, my wife and I lost six children at various stages of the pregnancies. I always wanted to be part of a child's life from their first day, and I looked forward to having grandchildren. When my diagnosis came with such gloomy odds of survival, it looked like I would never see that day. But thanks to the successful transplant, I have survived. The day I so dearly hoped for came April fifth when my grandson, Emerson, was born. I was able to meet him face to face because both of us were an example of miraculous God-given life—his new, and mine renewed with the gift from my donor.*
>
> *My father did not have to bury another one of his sons. My son did not lose his father in the prime of his life. And Emerson will know his grandfather through personal relationship, not just through photos and anecdotal stories.*

Dependence can be a beautiful invitation to go deeper with our Creator. Dependence on God became a surprising gift for my dad in a way that he never could have fathomed without such an extreme need in the first place. Admitting we need help is scary and makes us feel vulnerable. Many of us associate having a need with failure or inadequacy. Needing something beyond ourselves can look like weakness in our modern society. This way of thinking results in children growing up without role models who can teach them how to be dependent in healthy ways.

Thinking we need nothing from anyone is dangerous. The problem is that at some point, we all face a turn in our stories that is beyond our capacity to handle. When life becomes painful, our true character is exposed. Hardship shows us and others where we are strong and where we are weak. It puts on display the reality that we just don't have it together after all. Life is fragile and we are vulnerable, and sooner or later it lets us know how much we need others.

My dad's bone-marrow donor was a living, breathing reminder of the good news found in Jesus. The grace extended to have a second chance at life isn't earned or negotiated; it's simply received with a grateful and earnest heart.

My dad showed up for me.

The donor showed up for my dad.

God ran up the hill for you.

Whom are you showing up for?

By adopting you into his family, God passed a heritage of acceptance and love on to you. Your entire life is now devoted to living as he does—wholeheartedly and unabashedly searching for ways to extend unconditional love to others. This invitational life is all about sharing with those you meet the good news that there is a God who loves them, pursues them, and believes in them. A Christian life is lived without shame, fully exposed in our imperfections yet fully accepted as we are. The God of the universe loves us with a fierce fatherly love.

5
EVERYONE, ALWAYS

What makes God's heart beat?

In Romans 10:13, we find Paul writing to a little church in Rome, reminding them of what makes God's heart beat. He wanted to recast their vision of inclusivity and challenge them to expand their perspectives. Boldly he claimed, "Everyone who calls on the name of the Lord will be saved." *Everyone.*

Every Buckeyes fan who calls on the name of the Lord will be saved, along with every Republican, every Democrat, every immigrant, every Socialist, Communist, capitalist, every straight person, every gay person, every person you can't stand, every person you hate.

I don't know about you, but there are some ways of believing, living, and voting that are harder for me to accept than others. There are some people I fundamentally disagree with, and, honestly, some I generally dislike. So a statement like Paul's knocks the wind out of my puffed-up and small-minded self. It makes me uncomfortable in some ways. But in others, it comes at me like a slow, sweet sigh of relief. Because we don't have to be the ones to decide who is "in" and who is "out." According to Paul, God has decided that, and God says he's going to go ahead and let *everyone* who calls on him be saved. Which begs the question: How expansive is your view and invitation to love everyone?

I imagine this church in Rome sitting and listening as this letter was read to them. I wonder if they felt the same discomfort and agitation as they comprehended exactly what Paul was saying. They were eager to live as God desired, so they asked, "How do we do it? And to whom do we go?"

Paul responded in his brilliant rhetorical manner: "How, then, can they call on the one they have not believed in? And how can they believe in the one of whom they have not heard? And how can they hear without someone preaching to them? And how can anyone preach unless they are sent?" (Rom. 10:14–15).

Essentially Paul was saying, "If we want to be the kind of community that goes out to see every living, breathing person call on the name of the Lord, then we have to actually *go*. And people need to feel they've been sent. We'll need to step out of our comfort zones, leave the familiar, to risk and preach."

Nothing preaches more powerfully than your own story. When people hear about the deeply personal and unique ways God has redeemed and saved you, they might just believe. And when they believe, they might just call on the name of the Lord. You might be asking, "How do I know if I'm sent?" In Paul's way of thinking, once you've called on the name of the Lord and have been saved, you've in turn been sent. Is God your redeemer, rescuer, and savior? Congratulations, you just got sent.

EXPANDING THE INVITATION

We've all been sent out. But to whom? To everyone. To do what? To preach. To preach what? Our story—in hopes that anyone might listen and hear it. Tell of how you've tasted and seen God's goodness. Tell how you've experienced grace firsthand. And when people who hear your story call on the name of the Lord, they will then be sent to tell their own stories of God's grace and goodness. That's the inclusive, beautiful arc of God's kingdom. You might be saying, "Yeah, but what's in it for me?" "Yeah, but I don't want to be labeled as judgmental or seen as 'one of those people.'" "Yeah, but you don't know how many times I've tried and failed."

When it comes to a masterful incarnation of this invitational life, we need look only to Jesus. He understood the way in which followers of God should orient their lives. One time Jesus was seated around a table with a gathering of people, and he decided to tell them a story. He said, "A certain man was preparing a great banquet and invited many guests. At the time of the banquet he sent his servant to tell those who had been invited, 'Come, for everything is now ready'" (Luke 14:16–17).

The food was ready, the band had shown up, and it was time for a grand celebration. Come now and quickly. "But [the guests] all alike began to make excuses. The first said, 'I have just bought a field, and I must go and see it. Please excuse me.' Another said, 'I have just bought five yoke of oxen, and I'm on my way to try them out. Please excuse me'" (vv. 18–19). I've heard a lot of excuses in my day, but those are news ones for sure. And then, "Still another said, 'I just got married, so I can't come'" (v. 20).

So the servant went back and reported to his master. The master was angry that he had invited his friends, but they gave excuses and refused to come. Rejection can stop us in our tracks. It can shut us down and paralyze our momentum. The fear of rejection can be just as powerful, and in some cases even more so, because it keeps us from ever trying. But in the next part of the parable, the master used rejection as an opportunity to expand the servant's perspective of who could come to the table.

Every one of us has spheres of influence that stretch far beyond our immediate relationships. Think for a moment about the people God has placed in your life who would be open to your invitation. Perhaps they respect the grace you exude, the compassion you show, and the love you display. They may be waiting for you to make a simple invitation.

When I was in high school, a kid named Bryan sat several tables away from me in the lunchroom. He definitely wasn't "cool," and he kept mostly to himself. Often after my basketball practices, I would go to a nearby park to shoot hoops before heading home. Sometimes Bryan would show up at the park too, and we would shoot hoops and talk. Away from everybody else, I could be his friend. But at school I acted like I didn't know him. This is still something I deeply regret.

I remember when one of my mentors noticed me avoiding Bryan. He pulled me aside and said, "You know, your view of God's heart for humanity is narrow. You don't want to inconvenience your life, and you're afraid to invite someone from the outside in. So you just hang out with him on the side instead of bringing him into what you say matters most."

All are welcome. No matter who they are, it's our job to go find them and invite them in. That's why, in Jesus's parable, the master said to his servant, "Go out … and look for the poor, look for the crippled, look for the blind and lame. Go after them" (see v. 21). The servant went out and invited a number of these people to the party. When he came back, he told the master, "Some of them came, but there's still room at your banquet" (see v. 22).

So the master told his servant, "Go out to the roads and country lanes and compel them to come in, so that my house will be full" (v. 23). I love this, because here the master was essentially saying, "I want you to go to the far-off road, and then if there is still room at the banquet, I want you to go to every alley and find every person who is standing alone, every person who feels like an outsider, every person who feels unseen. I want you to show up out there and share your story, because you know what kind of party I throw."

Jesus told this story to reinforce the fact that in God's kingdom, everyone is welcome at the party. No one should be kept away. We know that Jesus put up with all sorts of ugly behaviors with grace and patience. But when people had a narrow view of "everyone," it infuriated him.

In Jesus's day, the temple was thirty acres of awe-inspiring glory—and was a sort of tourist attraction for people from all over. Travelers from the ancient Near East came to see it up close. It's likely that when people heard about King Herod's temple, they would have been in awe. But when they saw it with their own eyes, they would have left utterly amazed and giving reverence to God.

Imagine you and your family are on a pilgrimage from Egypt to see this temple with your own eyes. You've heard about it and have journeyed far to reach it. But because you are an outsider, you can enter only certain limited sections. On top of that, religious leaders have turned the sections available to you into an indoor bazaar.

You stand there, exhausted, thirsty, dusty, and aching to get close to the presence of God. But now your senses are overcome with braying livestock, yelling salesmen, and bartering customers. Little trinkets glimmer in the sun, and piles of blankets are stacked up on tables, making it impossible to see beyond the courtyard. You're standing outside the gates and can't get through. Jesus sees you through the crowd. In fact, he sees your family and the hundreds of people standing outside beside you as these religious leaders set up tables and count their money, oppressing people who desperately need to encounter God.

The Gospels tell us that Jesus became enraged and began flipping over tables while quoting Old Testament scriptures. In one passage, he said, "My [Father's] house will be called a house of prayer" (Mark. 11:17). It's easy to miss, but Jesus was doing something brilliant with this line. In the Jewish culture, most Hebrew people memorized the entire Old Testament. There was a technique called a *remez*, in which you would intentionally leave out key parts of a passage, and others would fill in the blanks and recite them back to you. Clever Jesus said, "My [Father's] house will be called a house of prayer," but he intentionally omitted the phrase "for all nations" (v. 17). The religious leaders had forgotten we all belong to each other. They had a narrow view of what "all nations" meant.

When Jesus started flipping over tables, he wasn't really angry about the money but more so the exploitation of people. He saw those who should be displaying God's inclusive character doing the exact opposite. People were prevented from worshipping God, and that provoked Jesus's anger. God understands that when believers gather with people searching for their faith, we're preparing ourselves for heaven—where every tribe, tongue, and nation will join together to praise our heavenly Father. The invitation into life with God through Jesus is for everyone, always.

SEEDS OF GRACE AND JOY

Recently my son and his grandpa made a small wooden birdhouse together. They hammered and painted and had it just right before hanging it on a tree in our backyard. My son anxiously stared at that birdhouse, hoping to get a glimpse of its new tenants. A few weeks went by, and no birds had shown up. Then my son had an idea. We went to the store and bought a big bag of birdseed. As soon as we got home, he dragged that bag to the yard, tore it open, and stuck his little hands in deep. Then he started running around the yard throwing seeds everywhere and laughing like a lunatic.

I want to live my life like that—to be free to delight in the moment, scattering seeds of love and grace everywhere I go. Sadly some of us are afraid there might be an end to grace, a limit to love. The truth is, you can't run out of seeds of grace and love.

You can't run away from grace or run out of it; it's everywhere you go. When you have seeds of grace, you can't help but spread them around. So how do we do this? What does it look like when we're at a coffee shop or in line at a bank? What do seeds of grace look like when we're in a conversation with a neighbor or when we're dropping our kids off at school?

First, as we learned in the previous section of this book, we live in deep appreciation and knowledge of God's gift of grace. Then we show up in the world and look for the good in others. We look for their need, and we relentlessly invite others to come and see God's love and grace on display.

What does it mean to look for the good in others? It means walking into any situation and making a conscious choice to focus on the positive attributes within a person. This may sound easy, and perhaps it is with certain people. But for so many years of my life as a follower of Jesus, it was hard for me to look for the good. Without giving it much thought, I'd focus on the things that made me different from other people—where they were from, how they dressed, what they were interested in, how they voted.

I looked for differences, and to be honest, what I was really doing was separating myself from them. I was looking for reasons to be apart; I was searching for excuses that would justify my lack of grace for them. In lots of ways, I was just looking for the bad to let me off the hook, to keep myself at a safe distance. I focused on the badness instead of the goodness because I didn't want to throw seeds of grace to those people. I was storing up my seeds, hoarding them, afraid they would run out if I gave them away.

The truth is, any situation we walk into has potential for eternal impact. All of humanity is in search of grace; we're all desperate for good news. As Christians we can be conduits of grace. We have the good news in our grasp, and we get to toss seeds of grace to those who are hungry for it.

DIG FOR THE GOLD

Looking for good is like digging for gold. We look for the good within a culture that is so cynical, so angry, and so judgmental that random acts of kindness are seen as out of the ordinary. There is a massive grace gap available for us to fill. We get to be a compelling force for grace, drawing out good and pointing people to what truly is good. We become like treasure hunters excitedly searching for the gold buried within the pain, the hope struggling to rise up from the ashes.

Recently I was in the airport ticket line when an announcement informed us that, regretfully, our flight would be delayed because of the weather. The passenger in front of me wasn't happy and let the airline representative know it. This guy's plans had been interrupted, and he was looking for someone to blame. Unfortunately that someone turned out to be the ticket agent behind the desk. He took all his frustration out on her, yelling and demanding she resolve the problem immediately. This scene was pretty embarrassing, and I felt uncomfortable witnessing the outburst.

Fortunately this agent responded brilliantly. Without getting defensive or snide, she let the angry traveler get it all off his chest. Then she took a deep breath, smiled, and began to calmly explain the problem in a way he seemed to understand. She put on a clinic for how to handle difficult people in a nondefensive way. She defused a challenging situation by asking the man questions and making a true connection.

When it was my turn at the counter, I spent a few moments affirming the woman and asked her, "Where did you learn to defuse such a hostile situation?" She began to tell me about her mother, whom she described as the strongest, kindest, and most faith-filled person she'd ever known. I replied, "Your mom would have been proud to see the strength, kindness, and faith you displayed today."

She started to tear up and told me that her mom had passed six months ago. Then she said, "I've never had my mom's faith, which is probably why it's been so hard to get through this." Just by showing up and looking for the good in an ordinary moment, I got a front-row seat to the ways God was at work in this woman's story.

Every person in your life has a story, and every story has the potential to be redeemed through the grace of God's unconditional love. When we say yes to Jesus, we say yes to grace—both receiving it and giving it. Looking for the good in another person is the best way to see glimpses of God in our daily lives.

When we scatter seeds of grace, we also have our eyes open for need. Every one of us has experienced pain, disappointment, bad decisions, betrayal, and fear at some point in our lives. No one is immune to suffering. Our struggles may manifest in different ways, from addictions to perfectionism to codependency. As Christians, we need to remember that when we encounter blatant sin or need, it isn't a red flag that gives us permission to withhold grace from others. The need, the sin, the brokenness are part of a person's story, which God is in the process of redeeming and making new.

For someone who is living outside the arms of grace, that's very good news. That pain you're living in? It's not the whole story. That hopelessness you can't climb out of? God isn't finished with you yet. That drug addict, homeless person, hypocrite, liar you cannot stand?

God is at work in each of them. The story isn't finished yet. We're in process, waiting for seeds of grace to turn the page.

I was at our local grocery store recently when a woman from our church approached me, excited to share something. She grabbed my arm and said, "I have to tell you one thing!"

"Okay, what is it?" I asked. Internally I felt a prompting to start throwing some seeds, extending grace, and searching for the good and the need in this woman's story.

"This past year has been the best year of my life," she exclaimed.

When I asked her why, she shared that she had started attending our church. I asked her how she came to attend, wondering if someone invited her. She said, "My family was going through trauma, and it was a really painful time for me. My sister-in-law has been a part of the church, and one day she asked me to come. I went, and the community welcomed me. And this has been the best year of my life."

I walked out of that grocery store, and as I got into my car, I was so grateful for this woman and her story. As amazing as it was to hear of the renewal in her life, I found myself thanking God for that sister-in-law who threw seeds of grace, searched for the good, and spoke into the need of her family member. She didn't use their differences as an excuse to avoid or judge; instead, she decided to pay attention to what was happening in her life. She didn't force anything; she simply invited her to come and see.

When you're looking for good and looking for need, you get the chance to winsomely invite someone to come and see, to be honest and human, to experience the grace of God. At the end of that Romans passage, Paul said, "How beautiful are the feet of those who bring good news" (10:15). How beautiful are the feet of those who scatter seeds of grace, who pay attention to the stories around them, who search for need and invite others to come and see how good our God is.

Welcome to this invitational life. Think of what might happen in your family, community, city, state, and even the world when we all participate. What places is God calling you into so that your view of everyone can be widened? What would it look like this week if every place you go, you look for the good and throw some seeds of grace? Here's the beautiful thing: by throwing seeds of grace toward others and paying attention to their stories, you're playing an active role in God's redemption of their lives. Everyone, always.

6
MASSEVOT

I will never forget the moment I first held my son, the precious seconds as I gazed down at him—his tiny hand, warm and fresh and perfectly new, gripping my finger so tightly. I was a wreck, of course. It was all so much to absorb, and there was a weight to the moment. It was heaven crashing into my world and rocking it forever. It was all so holy.

Sometimes all we can do is cry and try desperately to hang on to every part of a memory, so that as time goes by, the holiness of that experience doesn't fade. It's hard to hold on to the memories of a miracle, isn't it? We're such tactile people that we often need a physical expression to ingrain the memory for us.

Imagine you have just crossed the Red Sea. Your back is toward Egypt, the place of oppression and slavery. For the first time, you're free. Sure, you're exhausted, weary from the chase you've just survived. But your heart is racing and you're running on adrenaline thanks to the mind-blowing miracles you've just witnessed. There must have been all kinds of reactions happening in the moment after the sea swallowed up the Egyptian soldiers, after the slaves had a chance to take in what had just transpired. They were free. God had made it so.

From somewhere to your left, you hear a faint song rise up from the crowd. A woman called Miriam begins to sing an anthem. The chorus spreads, and soon the whole nation of Israel joins in this song about what they had just witnessed God doing. Sometimes nothing says it better than a song, and so a song becomes a way to mark a moment, to savor a miracle.

At other times, you commemorate a place by giving it a name. In Genesis 32, we read about Jacob in an all-night wrestling match with someone he thought was just a man. The next morning he realized he wasn't wrestling a man; he was wrestling God. And so he named the place *Peniel*, which means "face of God." As Jacob said, "I saw God face to face, and yet my life was spared" (v. 30). Sometimes you write a song; sometimes you name a place. But when you have an encounter with God, you find a way to remember it.

In Exodus 24, Moses climbed to the top of Mount Sinai to meet with God, who expressed his heart's desire for Israel to be his people. God, who had just rescued them from the darkest places, chose them and wanted to live with them. But he didn't demand it—he invited them into life with him. Moses hiked back down to where the newly freed Israelite people were waiting, and he asked them a question: Will you live as God's chosen people? They answer collectively, "We will" (see v. 3). A holy invitation was accepted.

In the morning Moses got up. He built an altar, where he sacrificed some animals. He set up twelve large stones, one to represent each of the twelve tribes of Israel. God responded, a miracle happened, and they marked the place so they would always remember.

Every one of these stones told a story of how God moved, but there's more to it. In Joshua 4 we read that the Hebrew people were situated on one side of the Jordan River. On the other side of the Jordan was the Promised Land—the land God promised to Abraham, Isaac, and Jacob. It's where the people were supposed to go after all those years of wandering. But how were they going to get there? The river was too dangerous to cross. So God directed them to have the priests holding the ark of the covenant step into the river. He promised he would stop the flow of the river, allowing the people to cross. They did this, and one by one all of the Israelites moved into the Promised Land.

While this is an amazing miracle, it's also a testament to God's faithfulness. After the Israelites crossed over the Jordan, God requested a memorial—because he knew his people needed help remembering. So Joshua called together the twelve men he had appointed from the Israelites, one from each tribe, and said to them,

> Each of you is to take up a stone on his shoulder, according to the number of the tribes of the Israelites, to serve as a sign among you. In the future, when your children ask you, "What do these stones mean?" tell them that the flow of the Jordan was cut off before the ark of the covenant of the LORD. When it crossed the Jordan, the waters of the Jordan were cut off. These stones are to be a memorial to the people of Israel forever. (Josh. 4:5–7)

As people would pass by these stones in ancient Israel and Palestine, they would ask the question, "What do these stones mean?" The word they used for "stones" was *massevot*, and it became a shorthand way of saying, "What happened here?"[1]

Peter was a disciple of Jesus who took this concept even further. He wrote,

> As you come to him, the living Stone [Jesus]— rejected by humans but chosen by God and precious to him—you also [the church], like living stones, are being built into a spiritual house to be a holy priesthood, offering spiritual sacrifices acceptable to God through Jesus Christ. (1 Pet. 2:4–5)

Right away Peter established this concept of the *massevot* stones: "I want you to understand that you are living stones." He went on to say, "You are a chosen people, a royal priesthood, a holy nation, God's special possession, that you may declare the praises of him who called you out of darkness into his wonderful light" (v. 9). He's saying you are a treasured possession of the almighty God. You belong to his family. You have been chosen.

SHOW UP AND BE SEEN

You are a living stone with a story to tell about how you have been redeemed and restored. Peter said that as living stones, we should live such good lives that others will see our good deeds and glorify God (see 1 Pet. 2:12). This phrase *good deeds* in Hebrew is the word *mitzvah*, which refers to sacred, God-oriented deeds. The idea being that people who are far from God will see the way you orient your life and will want to know more.

The way you live your life should invoke a curiosity in everyone you meet. This curiosity about the choices you make, the peace you offer, the wisdom you display, and the love you exude should cause them to ask, "*Massevot*—what's happened there?" Your life can sing the praises of the One who redeemed and restored you. The ways you interact in the various environments can be so compelling that people will want to know why you're choosing to live that way.

A number of years ago, I met Austin, a sixth grader who loved the game of basketball. He was just your average kid, funny and good and kind of a goofball. One day God got ahold of his heart after he'd learned that 2,452 kids across the world are orphaned every day from HIV/AIDS. Later that year, on World AIDS Day, Austin started Hoops for Hope and committed to shoot 2,452 free throws in an effort to raise money to help change the story. On December 1, 2004, he took his jump shot and started shooting free throws. That year he raised $3,000.

News of this event traveled, and soon other students from all over the country began to join in. In 2006 Austin raised $85,000 and funded the construction of a school in Zambia. An ordinary junior high student built a school in Zambia for orphans by shooting free throws.

But wait—it gets better! The next year Austin said, "I've got bigger dreams. I want to add a health clinic to the school in Zambia." Even more people joined the effort from across the country, and together they raised $211,000. During halftime at the NCAA Final Four tournament, CBS did a special documentary. They had Ashley Judd interview Austin, and in six minutes he succinctly explained the story behind his campaign.[2] Essentially he was being asked, "*Massevot*, Austin? What's happened here?"

Right in the middle of a nationally televised sporting event, Austin told about the hope that's found in Jesus. Talk about being a living stone. I love this story because it started so innocently with a kid who saw a need and found a creative way to respond.

I wish more people would ask me "*Massevot?*" so I could tell them about the hope I have. I mentioned this to a friend of mine. He replied, "Well, either your life is too safe or you hang out with too many Christians or your life isn't that compelling."

Ouch! But thank you. The truth hurts sometimes, doesn't it?

When was the last time someone looked at you and said, "*Massevot*—what happened here?" When was the last time people noticed the love, grace, and joy emanating from you so naturally that they had to ask you why. What sets you apart, what makes you different, what is it about your daily interactions with others that leads them closer to Jesus?

The Christian life can be lived in such a way that it demands an explanation. So how do we get there? As we talked about earlier, we start by living intentionally and going deep with Jesus. To live intentionally is to wake up and say, *God, help me be more aware of your presence. If my life is going to demand an explanation, I need you to pour yourself into me so that I have miracles to remember. Remind me of the times you have been faithful and miraculous in my life.* We continue to spend time reading God's Word every single day. When we spend time with Jesus, we invite him to develop our character to mirror his. As we strive to become more Christlike, we can go out into our environments each day asking God to teach us something new about who he is and who he calls us to be. The Holy Spirit does the work of making our inner and outer selves more like Jesus; that is, more able to love without condition. Then we show up, every day, ready for God to use us to reach the lost among us.

LIVING STONES

We live intentionally when we show up with great expectancy. The greatest risk takers I know have identified specific faces and places they're called to pray for. They would call themselves the pastors of those places. They would say, "You know that coffee shop (or restaurant or gym) around the corner? I go there often, and I care about the people there. I know the staff by name, and I'm getting to know their stories."

A friend of mine who takes the train into the city for work shared that every morning he prays for the person who will be seated next to him. He prays for the chance to learn that individual's story and the chance to tell God's story.

The presence of God is everywhere. There is redemptive potential in every place you go, because God is there. When you realize that and decide you want to show up too, miracles happen. Lives are changed. Living this way will change the way you pray. You're expectant. You're on your toes. You're eager to discover how God is going to work in the environment you're in, and you anticipate opportunities to join him.

If you were to ask my wife about my handyman skills, she might just start laughing hysterically. I don't know anything when it comes to fixing up our house. So naturally, one of the scariest places for me is Home Depot. It's a place that shines a giant spotlight on my weaknesses and inability. The truth is, I didn't get the chance to learn those skills when I was younger, so I grew up without knowing how to fix even the simplest things.

I know when I walk through those doors, I'm going to have find someone in an orange apron and admit that I don't know what I'm doing. So my prayer every time I enter Home Depot is, *Lord, will you father me through this?*[3] With this perspective, I enter the store with a teachable heart. I want to learn, and so I seek out someone who can teach me. And every time, I find someone who is kind and patient, willing to coach me and convince me that I actually can do it.

Striking up a conversation with a perfect stranger can be awkward and scary. If you're nervous about it, consider praying a similar prayer before you walk into an environment where God might prompt you to connect with someone new. Say to God, *Lord, would you father me through this? Would you give me your heart, your eyes? Please allow me to have conversations that will encourage people to keep searching for you.*

We get to *massevot* when we spark ongoing relationships. I love the word *ongoing*, because it's not just a one-and-done thing. Building relationships isn't something you do and check off a list. It's a marathon that has potential to last a lifetime. You're not supposed to become a slick salesperson who slides in to close a deal. You're looking for where you can build consistency. Make the most of every opportunity. Walk into the places you've been praying about, expecting opportunities to strike up grace-filled conversations.

The next question you can ask God as you're building relationships with the people you've been praying for is this: "What is the next best right step for these people? I know their names. I know their stories. Is the right step to invite them to church? Is it to invite them to my house for dinner? Is it to tell them my story? Is it to tell them God's story?"

There's a world of hurting, confused people out there. I want to risk myself to reach as many as I can. How about you? Let's be bold. Let's be fearless with our faith. When I say risk boldly, I don't mean risk loudly or risk obnoxiously. Risk with grace and truth. Ask God for opportunities to declare fearlessly, with love and compassion, the reality of the good news.

If we're honest, many of us enter into these environments as silent stones. We just want to order our coffee and leave. Maybe we hope someone will stop us and ask us to tell them about Jesus. Maybe we hope that if they don't ask us, we'll be let off the hook. But it doesn't happen that way. We're all called to be living stones, boldly proclaiming through our lives that God is good and true. The people we encounter need to see how life with Jesus changes everything. We have to be vulnerable and open.

The ground at the foot of the cross is level, and anyone can come to receive Jesus. We get to be the mouthpieces of God's story. It's not just our responsibility; it's our honor and privilege. God entrusted his story to us. Wherever the Spirit is calling you, would you be so bold to take a risk and say, "Here I am, God; send me"? That is one of the most powerful prayers throughout the Scriptures. If you're willing to take that risk, God wants to use you, and he will. Specific people in your life right now need someone to take a risk with them, as someone took a risk with you.

There's no greater joy, no greater honor, and nothing more fulfilling than witnessing another person receive the gospel. You can't
touch someone else's life for good without having your own impacted
just as much, if not more.

While in college I worked part time busing tables at a local
pub. One night a group of five servers came up to me and said,
"There's something different about you. What is it?" A wave of fear
came over me for a moment as I imagined what would happen if
I actually told them the truth—that my life completely changed
because of Jesus. I wondered, *If I tell them about my faith, will it
change my relationship with them? What if they write me off as a crazy
Christian, and I lose my chance to influence them?* The apostle Peter
said, "Always be prepared to give an answer to everyone who asks
you to give the reason for the hope that you have" (1 Pet. 3:15). It's
as if Peter expects that our lives will demand an explanation. He
counsels us to be ready when the questions come, ready to share
what our hope is all about.

I guess maybe I felt a rush of boldness in the moment, because
before I could overthink it too much, I told them about my faith. I
let them know about the One who guides my life, the reason for the
way I interacted and reacted in their presence. And you know what?
There was no drama, no mocking, and no weird looks. But there
also weren't instant conversions. No one kneeled and prayed. We just
went on with our work. The twist is, throughout the evening I had
two separate conversations with fellow servers who had questions
about Jesus. This led to months of ongoing, informal talks about
faith and what it means to be a Christian. Later, both of these servers
accepted Jesus's invitation to follow him as Savior.

Never underestimate your influence in a certain context. We have no idea about the inner workings of Christ within and among us. We have a choice to make, of course. We can be silent stones or living stones. When someone asks you what makes you different, you need to decide what kind of stone you will be—silent and secret or living and inviting.

7
DELIBERATELY INTENTIONAL

My friend is a sommelier, and I'll admit I didn't understand what that meant for the longest time. I thought it meant he was French. Don't worry—I get it now. He has vast knowledge of wines and where they are produced. Blindfold him and give him a taste of wine, and he can tell you not only the kind of wine it is but also the exact vineyard off the coast of Spain where it was made. When I express my amazement at his ability, his response is, "It takes a lot of practice to differentiate the tastes."

I have another friend who is a musician. His ear has been trained since he was a kid to hear every element of a song. When I listen to music, I hear the song as a whole. I like the vibe, the soul, and the way it makes me feel. For him, it's a completely different experience. His ear breaks down every aspect—every strum, tick, beat, dip, and swing. For him, it's taken a lifetime of training to acquire his ability to assess and savor every note. Consequently, this skill enables him to craft some of the most beautiful and rich melodies I've ever heard.

Once you learn the sound—or smell or taste—of something, it stays with you. It's as though it becomes a part of you, and you never unlearn it.

I vividly remember the gym from the movie *Hoosiers*. It was iconic. The hardwood floors, the creaky bleachers, the hazy light filtering dramatically through the dirty windows. That was definitely a place where sports legends could come from. The gym I used to play basketball in as a kid had that same feel to it. Ironically enough, what I remember most about that place was the humming sound of the fluorescent lights. It was a low buzz, annoying at first, but after a while it became part of what made that place feel legendary in my mind. I think back fondly to the sounds of those lights, the whistles of the coaches, and the squeaks of our shoes on the floor as we ran our drills.

We've talked about how God's presence is everywhere. We believe that the Holy Spirit is diligently at work trying to illuminate Christ and draw all people back to God. He does this sometimes by speaking to you and me. Which means every situation we encounter is brimming with possibility. The sounds of redemption are all around us. Once we learn to recognize them, our lives are never the same. We can train ourselves to be attuned to the Spirit's nudges and God's still, small voice.

How open and available are you to hear God throughout your day? Is hearing God's voice something you practice, or is it new to you?

For much of my life, I was pretty closed off to the Holy Spirit's promptings. I would enter a restaurant looking to get something quick and leave. I'd be unaware of who served me—the person's name—and what God wanted me to do. I struggled to show up. I wasn't fully present to what was happening around me. Showing up is all about a deeper interior motivation. A mentor of mine used to say, "Be deliberately intentional." Showing up is being supremely focused on what the Spirit of God is longing to accomplish in your midst. When you are deliberately intentional and supremely focused on what is stirring all around you, you become available for God's redemptive purposes.

LISTEN AND BE LED

Recently, while I was reading Jesus's baptism story in the book of Matthew, I was blown away by these words: "Then Jesus was led by the Spirit into the wilderness" (4:1). Jesus went public with his faith, and the love of God was sealed over him before he ever healed someone or preached a message. How beautiful is that? God loves you unconditionally not because of any accomplishment you think makes you valid and worthy of love, but because you are you.

After the sealing of his love, the Spirit sent Jesus out. We see this sending of the Spirit throughout the New Testament. The Spirit prompted Peter to have "no hesitation" to enter a Gentile's house. A similar thing happened with Paul and Barnabas, as the Holy Spirit sent them out and led them to city after city to share the invitation. The book of Acts is this collection of stories showcasing ways in which the Spirit of God was on the move. The characters in the New Testament understood that God was up to something good, and they knew he was inviting them to join the fun.

Which makes me wonder: When was the last time you felt the Spirit sending you? When was the last time you entered a place with the belief that God was already up to something? When was the last time you heard the Holy Spirit whisper to you and you followed through on it? When we live like this, we start showing up to our lives and the environments we inhabit with an expectant posture.

Expectancy is the birthplace of dependency on God. It's here you begin to learn what the voice of God sounds like. It's here where your ears and heart are open to God. Your approach to daily activities changes. Just running to the store for laundry detergent and toothpaste? Nope. You're carrying your story with you into a place where God is already at work. Making a quick deposit at the bank on your way home from work? Nope. You're partnering with God in the renewal of everything.

So we go into various places, expectant that God will show us where we can partner with him. We're listening for that inner prompting. Perhaps it's a sense or a word or a specific urge to pray. There are many internal ways the Spirit can speak to us. When that prompting comes, we have the choice to respond or not. Our faith grows when we respond to the promptings of God. If we hear him and do nothing, we miss a chance to grow nearer to him. We miss a chance to grow more dependent on him.

Hearing begins with showing up expectant, hungry, and looking for what God is up to. My friend Aaron created a refrain he sings at the beginning of his worship set each weekend that says, "Speak, LORD, for your servant is listening" (1 Sam. 3:9). We start with listening. We wait for what the Lord might say. We respond. We act. We pray. We lead.

I don't want to miss out on the moments when God wants to use me. Sometimes something keeps us from saying a big, wild *yes* when we hear his voice. Perhaps fear holds us back.

We don't want to be pushy.

We don't want to feel awkward.

We don't feel qualified.

We aren't sure we have anything to offer.

We question if we actually heard his voice.

We want to be liked, we want to be comfortable, and we want to feel confident. But at the heart of it, we're afraid we're not enough, and we don't trust that God will provide what we need if we take a risk. God is always there for his children. He never fails us. When we go where he asks us to go, he will always meet us there. He'll open doors, prepare hearts, and give us words to speak.

We can't control the way others respond when we reach out to them. That part is up to them. We *can* control the way we approach and engage. We can trust that we have what it takes because we're gifted with characteristics of the very nature of God, and we can trust that above all, we have the best news to offer.

In Acts 13, five people gathered to pray in a room in Antioch. These five represent how wide the good news had spread. You have Manaen, who was raised in King Herod's house and brought up with his kids. He saw firsthand the power, ambition, and fear that gripped Herod's life. You have Simeon and Lucius of Cyrene, whom scholars believe were from northern Africa, and you have Barnabas from Cyprus and Saul. This prayer circle represented how the gospel was spreading to the ends of the earth.

As the five of them were worshipping, praying, and fasting, the Holy Spirit spoke: "Set apart for me Barnabas and Saul for the work to which I have called them" (v. 2). When these five fully showed up, they heard the sounds of redemption breaking in. It's the kind of vision that could not be ignored, where the Holy Spirit beckoned them to leave the familiar and enter the unknown.

This is the story of the first missionary journey Paul and Barnabas embarked on. Can you imagine if they hadn't shown up, fully present, to that meeting? What an adventure they would have missed. How many people would have missed out on the beautiful invitation into life with God?

How many people will miss out on the invitation if you don't show up in their lives? But sometimes, as followers of Jesus, we get confused about what our roles are with others who don't believe like we do. Sometimes we think it's our job to be right. We think it's our responsibility to defend the gospel. We go around looking for chances to prove our faith or try to argue others out of theirs. But when interacting with people one on one, we would be wise to listen before speaking. Listen for God's redemptive purposes, and listen to the other person share his or her story or perspective.

Many of us struggle with listening to the Spirit and to one another. When we don't listen, our best intentions manifest in a conversation as an agenda. We forget to look at the other person as someone who deserves to be heard. Studies show that "humans generally listen at a 25 percent comprehension rate."[1] That means 75 percent of what people share is floating in some other galaxy, because we're grabbing for our phones or already focused on giving a rebuttal. I often wonder if this is why so many people struggle with sharing the invitation—because they've lost the art of listening well. Another interesting stat tells us that "85 percent of what you know you learned from listening."[2] The better the listener, the smarter the person. The better the listener, the stronger the invitation.

When we long to hear the Spirit, and we're deliberately intentional about learning from him, we are also training ourselves to listen well to others. Through an experience with the Alpha Course, a worldwide study program and movement started by Nicky Gumbel, I learned to listen in a new way. I began to ask more questions and focus more intently on the response of the other person. This took the pressure off me having to be right about everything. I learned to zero in on the other person rather than on myself. You might be surprised to see what happens when you do this yourself. If you listen to people, they'll think you're the interesting one, and they'll be more open to hearing from you when it's time for you to speak up.

HOLY EXPECTANCY

My wife and I led an Alpha Course group almost ten years ago. Every week our group grew. We had people who wanted nothing to do with God sitting beside people who had walked away from their faith. People who wanted to understand what the Christian faith meant had conversations with people who had been baptized decades before and drifted away. All these different people became raving evangelists for this Tuesday-night meeting, telling their friends, neighbors, and coworkers to come and see.

The Alpha Course recommends hosting a weekend retreat seven weeks into the program to teach people about the Holy Spirit. The word *spirit* can be a little daunting. It can seem mystical, cultish, or at the very least irrelevant for our modern society. It's easy to approach Christianity like that, because we like concrete ideas and something tangible to hold on to.

The Spirit is our counselor, who requires spiritual discipleship to actively engage with. The Spirit is the guide Jesus provided to lead us in love when he ascended into heaven. The Spirit whispers to our souls about where and who and how and when God is moving in and around and through us. If we aren't engaged in life with the Spirit, we aren't growing.

During our Alpha group retreat, the sounds of redemption came bursting forth, and during the worship and prayer time, we were able to hear what God was stirring in each person. I didn't give any answers; I just waited intentionally and prayerfully for what others had to share. As people spoke, I listened to the struggle in each person's life—and also to the whispers of the Holy Spirit.

God's nearness was palpable. The prayers were heartfelt and honest. There was a weight to the words that were spoken. Several people made decisions to follow Jesus for all of their days. Bearing witness to all that holy redemption blessed my faith like few things ever have. Just as in Acts 13, it all began by making space to listen well—to listen with a holy expectancy and the willingness to relentlessly follow those promptings as quickly as possible.

One of my favorite things to do is sit with people who are wrestling with questions about God. They're people who are genuinely exploring their doubts, frustrations, and hang-ups. Recently I sat with Chad and asked if he could specifically name the biggest obstacle to having a relationship with Jesus. He responded quickly, "My dad." After he said it, his entire posture changed, as if he had just voiced the thing that had been controlling his life.

I could sense the Holy Spirit prompting me to affirm what he shared, so I asked, "What are you feeling right now?"

He said, "Anger, sadness, and anxiety."

As we processed more and more, he began to open up about the pain he endured at the hands of his father. Over the next few months, we met regularly and continued to work through the pain in his story. At one point he felt ready to confront his father, surrender his life to Christ, and get baptized. To this day I'm so thankful for how that one question led Chad to be vulnerable and name what was stopping him from experiencing grace.

Next time you're with someone who doesn't know the Lord, start by showing up. Mentally remind yourself to focus on listening well and be deliberately intentional in your interactions. Be curiously engaged in what is being said. Care about what the person is going through. Look for the good and be open to what you might learn. And while you listen, be expectant about the Spirit's leading. Just imagine what God might stir in you, through you, and all around you.

PART III
RELATE

8
DOMINATE

I didn't grow up in a religious home. On Easter my parents often took me to the horse track. I grew up thinking "Resurrection" was the name of a horse, not a life-changing event. For some reason, my parents decided to put me in a well-respected Christian parochial school that was affiliated with a church. The school was great, the teachers were kind, and most of the students were friendly.

When I was in seventh grade, my life changed forever. There were two high school juniors who were the superstars of the school. They were hilarious, popular, and everyone wanted to be like them. Their names were Dominic and Nathan, but they usually went by the collective name Dominate.

One day after school, I saw Dominic walking toward me. I got a little nervous until he said, "Hey, Carter, do you want to learn how to *dominate* life?"

To this day that is the single greatest question anyone has ever asked me. Over the next few years, these two guys took me under their wings. They took a genuine interest in me, asking me questions and teaching me how to live. They invited me to play basketball and were the first to ever invite me to church. Dominic and Nathan were the first people I had encountered who were truly trying to live like Christ. It was my first encounter with the invitational life. Within a few months of hanging out with Dominate, I became a follower of Christ.

It all started with a relationship. Dominic and Nathan were willing to align themselves more with God's heartbeat than trying to maintain status. High school students often avoid junior highers, but not these two. I often wonder what my life would have looked like if Dominic had never asked me that question. From that time on, I kept these words in the forefront of my mind: "Follow my example, as I follow the example of Christ" (1 Cor. 11:1). When I didn't know what to do as a new Christ follower, I'd think about how Dominate would have chosen to act. I saw firsthand their willingness to use their influence for good, to cross social barriers to create relationships, and to seek every opportunity to talk about Christ. They truly taught me how to dominate life.

Earlier we talked about when Paul and Barnabas traveled to Pisidian Antioch. In Acts 13, the Holy Spirit said, "Set apart for me Barnabas and Saul for the work to which I have called them" (v. 2). It's interesting that when Paul started out on his first trip, he went by the name of Saul. That is, until he met a governor named Sergius Paulus, who was an intelligent man and not easily fooled. He invited Barnabas and Saul to visit him because he wanted to hear the gospel of God. But a sorcerer named Elymas tried to interfere and prevent the governor from believing what Barnabas and Saul said. Saul put this guy in his place, saying he was "an enemy of everything that is right!" (v. 10). The sorcerer was blinded, with Sergius Paulus looking on (see vv. 6–11).

Saul preached his first sermon ever, and a miracle took place, leaving the governor in awe. The Scriptures say, "When the [governor] saw what had happened, he believed, for he was amazed at the teaching about the Lord" (v. 12). From this time on, Saul became known as Paul. Some scholars say that Saul took the name Paul in honor of the first person who accepted his invitation to know Christ.

If what scholars say is true about Saul becoming Paul, then Dominate (Dominic and Nathan) would have taken my name. Who would have taken your name? Who made the first invitation to you?

I remember the first person I invited to know Jesus. I remember the first person I invited to church with me who actually said yes. I remember the first person I was able to baptize. My name could be Alex. What could your name be?

The lives of the first Christians we read about in Acts were transformed because of an intentional relationship and a simple invitation. I've noticed that we often make things more complicated than they need to be. We use a mind trick on ourselves by putting so much weight and pressure on us. We stress ourselves out by thinking we have to say everything perfectly. Our job is solely about relating and inviting. That's all we can do. The rest is up to God.

CITIZENS AND AMBASSADORS OF HEAVEN

It helps to consider ourselves as ambassadors of heaven. As Christians we carry the name of Christ into every environment we enter. That includes our relational environments. Through our behaviors, words, and actions, we show those who don't know Jesus what he looks like.

Did you know that Benjamin Franklin was a US ambassador? In December 1776, six months after the Declaration of Independence was signed, Franklin was sent to France. During this time there were two superpowers: England and France. These two monarchies had very different views of how government should be run. The brand-new United States was, of course, on England's bad side at that point in history. As a result, the United States was eager to win France's favor and resources. So our country decided to send a representative to France, someone with an esteemed reputation and skills in diplomacy. Ben Franklin fit the bill.

Franklin did a few brilliant things as he set out to become the first US ambassador to a foreign country. First, he chose to live in a smaller town outside of Paris called Passy—a perfect place to acclimate and avoid standing out too much. While he was there, he devoted himself to learning the French language. He studied the culture and developed relationships with his neighbors and the local vendors. Within no time, the French came to love him. They appreciated his curiosity and intellect. They loved the questions he asked. They valued his speaking to them in their own language.

After a time of intentionally relating to the people he was there to win over, Franklin persuaded the French to join in the States' fight for independence. France provided financial resources and troops to aid in the war so that the United States could defeat Great Britain. Scholars say that if it weren't for the diplomacy of Benjamin Franklin, the United States probably wouldn't have won the Revolutionary

War. To this day, Franklin is beloved in France, and he is one of the most revered statesmen in our country's history.

So what makes a good ambassador? What makes someone renowned for serving in this role? A good ambassador is someone who is loyal—loyal to the king, the prime minister, or the president. He or she is also loyal to the home country or kingdom.

Choosing to become ambassadors means choosing to align ourselves with another's set of values. To devote ourselves to that level of commitment, we must be passionate about the principles and beliefs of the kingdom we're representing. We have to embrace the ideals in a deep way. The buy-in goes beyond intellect and sinks into a way of being, and a way of the heart and the soul as well.

To represent a set of values well, we must put them ahead of any personal agenda. We must make ourselves humble enough to submit to those values. The word *humble* comes from the Latin word *humus*, which means "soil from the ground." To be humble is to be low like the ground. Jesus often talked about the ways a good life grows out of good soil. In the same way, a good life develops out of a humble approach. From humility, something good can take root, grow, blossom, and thrive.

When we enter into a new environment, do we come with an agenda? Do we come ready to deliver our opinions? Do we come thinking we have it all figured out? Or do we come low like the ground, humble yet solid in our convictions? When we begin the work of the invitational life, we open ourselves up to ambassadorship. First, we're inviting God to set the values we will honor and represent. We submit to his authority and leadership, and we humble ourselves so that we can put him first. Stepping into relationships with people who do things differently, speak differently, or believe differently works only if we're centered in God's values and humbled to relinquish our own judgments.

Without the looming internal distraction of judgment, we can better see the person behind the lifestyle. We can look at that person with the eyes of heaven, the place we're ultimately representing. With God's eyes, we may find we notice things about a person that we didn't before. In the past, someone's unpredictable temper may have put you off; now you see someone who is hurting. Then you can get to the work of Jesus—you can get curious. Why is the person angry? What's beneath all of that negative energy? You aren't coming with an agenda—you're sitting with that individual and asking great questions. Humility makes you accessible, and accessibility is good soil for planting seeds of grace.

When you get the chance to partner with God in what matters most to him, you recognize the privilege. Inviting people into a life of grace through Jesus and watching them say yes, watching them change and grow and develop, is easily one of the most thrilling, satisfying, and moving experiences we can have in life. We can't help but feel humbled that God would allow us to participate in his plans.

A TRIP TO SIN CITY

God sent the newly renamed apostle Paul to establish churches, and his work of teaching and developing was already under way when he visited a city called Corinth. Imagine Corinth as an emerging, bustling city that some scholars liken to Las Vegas. In fact, in Paul's day it was referred to as "Sin City." The term *corinthianize* meant "to corrupt a person, to take them past their moral limit."[1] Hundreds of thousands of people would come into the city almost as a rite of passage. People would do a number of perverse things there. You might say, "What happened in Corinth stayed in Corinth."

Miraculously, a church was being built in the epicenter of this perversion and brokenness. Paul came to instill a renewed sense of identity and responsibility in the Christians there. He told them in essence, "Friends, I want you to understand a couple of things: You are a new creation. The old, the past, all of those labels that have been handed to you—they're all gone. Because of Christ, the new is here. You are emerging and becoming something entirely different" (see 2 Cor. 5:17).

If anyone had the authority to speak about being made new, it was certainly Paul. He went on to say,

> All this is from God, who reconciled us to himself through Christ and gave us the ministry of reconciliation: that God was reconciling the world to himself in Christ, not counting people's sins against them. And he has committed to us the message of reconciliation. We are therefore Christ's ambassadors, as though God were making his appeal through us. We implore you on Christ's behalf: Be reconciled to God. (vv. 18–20)

Paul was telling this Corinthian church, "Since you've been made right with God, you've got a role to play. You are now ambassadors for the same God who saved you." As he said to the believers in Philippi, "[You] are citizens of heaven" (Phil. 3:20 NLT).

Your identity as a Christ follower first and foremost is as a citizen of heaven. You're a part of the commonwealth of eternity. This is who you are. The old is gone; the new is here. Because of that, you're here on Earth for a reason. You're in your city for a reason. You're in your school for a reason. You're on that team for a reason. You're sitting in that cubicle Monday through Friday for a reason. You live in that house for a reason. You go to that coffee shop for a reason. You are here for a reason: to be Christ's ambassador. You stand as an ambassador, representing your King wherever you go.

When we join the community of Christ, we become part of a great tradition of invitation. Someone invited you into God's loving family, and now you get to do the same. It will require leaning into your own grace story, overcoming fear, and stepping out with courage. Remember, the good news is for everyone, always. You can go public with your faith so that people longing for grace can find it.

The Holy Spirit has empowered you as an ambassador to carry the authority of Christ wherever you go. You get the supreme honor of participating with God as he transforms lives through love. When you commit to living this way, building authentic relationships and introducing others to Jesus and his peace, you just may end up with a new name!

9
CURIOUS

On an average weeknight in the neighborhood where I grew up, you could find about ten of us kids preparing for an epic game of hide-and-seek. We were serious about the game. Strategies were involved. Whenever I was riding in our car and we'd turn onto my street, I'd look out the window and plot my next hiding spot.

One night as my friend Cam started counting, we took off running to hide. I dashed for my latest perfect hiding spot—the back of Mr. Kawaguchi's work truck. I climbed over the side rail and lay down in the truck bed as still as I could. I'd been there, motionless, for a good ten minutes when I heard footsteps approaching the truck. I stayed frozen—and then I heard the sound of keys jiggling. Then the door opened. Then it closed. I waited, slowly catching on that this was not Cam discovering me. Then the engine fired up. Uh-oh.

At this moment I had a choice: I could jump up and scare Mr. Kawaguchi into a potential heart attack or keep hiding and see where he was going at nine o'clock on a Thursday night.

I've always been a curious guy, so I chose the latter. I lay low in the back of the pickup as he drove. I spent the entire drive imagining all the cool places he could be going. Vegas? San Francisco? The movies? Maybe he worked for the CIA, and I would blow his cover. Alas, we arrived at the local grocery store.

After a few minutes in the store, Mr. Kawaguchi walked back to his truck with a bag in his hand, opened the door, and drove back home. By the time we got back, my friends had given up on finding me (which is a sure sign of winning at hide-and-seek, right?). I was happy because that meant I didn't have to be the seeker in the next round.

Isn't it interesting that most of us would rather be the hiders than the seeker?

I wonder if our tendency to hide suggests something about humanity in general. Adam and Eve handed us a legacy of hiding. For much of my life, I hid key parts of my story. I was afraid that if people knew my struggles, if my weaknesses were exposed for all to see, it would cause them to avoid me. Deeper fear whispered that if I were found out, I would be rendered useless for the kingdom.

When we begin to build a relationship with someone new, the early points of connection are safer, less personal, and less threatening. As we grow in life together, our desire for connection deepens and beckons that we share the harder stuff with each other. Many of us don't ever reach this stage, or if we do, we're quick to sabotage it, eager for a way out. It feels so risky, so vulnerable, and leaves us open to the judgment and attack of others. So we just don't go there. We keep things light and superficial. Or we run away and hide.

God is always searching for us, calling out to us, and inviting us to step back into sight. He desires deep, true connection and knows his path leads us through the pain, not around it. When we let others see our weaknesses, it gives them permission to do the same. Stepping out of hiding, we've just given them the same gift of being seen and known that God has already given us.

Jesus invites us into a ridiculously curious kind of faith. He says, "Seek first [God's] kingdom" (Matt. 6:33). This word *seek* in Greek is *zeteo*, which has some fascinating nuances. The tense of the word suggests it is *an action that never ceases*. The word is used in the second person present active imperfect form—meaning there's an assumed understanding that it hasn't been completed yet.

So you could translate Matthew 6:33 as "continuously *seek*, without ever ceasing, the kingdom of God that hasn't been fully completed yet." There isn't an inch of this earth that God's presence doesn't inhabit. Everywhere we go, the kingdom of God is itching to burst forth in all its fullness. Peace. Healing. Reconciliation. Redemption. Love. All are yearning to be drawn out into the open.

It's safe to say that most people are living their lives in hiding, on the run, hoping they won't be found out. Yet it's also safe to say we all deeply desire to be fully known and seen. As Christians we know we're here on Earth for more than a lifetime of adventure or suffering. We're here to know God and make him known. We have an incredible opportunity to learn and encourage others to live bravely.

Whenever we encourage other people, we're instilling courage in them. We're telling them they have what it takes. We're telling them it's possible—regardless of what they're hiding from—to live their lives to the fullest expression of who God made them to be. Jesus lived this way. We can too. We need each other, because sometimes it's scary to come out of hiding, and sometimes we can't do it alone.

We need someone to speak truth to us. We need someone to instill courage in our hearts, so we can step out from behind the bush and stand face to face once again with our good God.

Each of us has potential to be filled with a holy curiosity to discover what God is up to. When we're lost, we spend our energies, talents, time, and resources desperately seeking what will make us feel like we're home again. When we find God and experience our own homecoming into his kingdom of grace, it's only natural to want to partner with him to seek those who are still lost.

The choice is ours. Hide or seek?

Our society is good at finding counterfeits to hide behind. There are plenty of things that promise to make up for what we're lacking. Money. Sex. Security. Physical appearance. Labels. Stuff. These things aren't bad, but they can be dangerous when they become the bushes we hide behind and keep us from living authentically with Christ. They can so easily become the measuring sticks that define our worthiness of being loved.

WHICH ANANIAS ARE YOU?

The book of Acts tells of two different men named Ananias. The first Ananias we encounter is a man swept up in what God was doing after Pentecost. He declared that he would sell a piece of property and give it to the church so people could have bread and pay their taxes to the Roman Empire. Then the proceeds came, and they were higher than expected. Ananias decided he didn't want to part with all of this money, so he ended up giving away only a portion of the funds.

A heart wide open to what God was doing let fear and greed creep in. At the end of the day, he chose the safer option, which is often the antithesis to the way of Jesus. He chose security, money, and dependency on himself rather than giving without fear, fully trusting that God would provide. He hid, and it didn't end well.

There have been so many moments in my life when my willingness to seek and risk has stalled because of fear. Fear that there won't be enough to go around. Fear about what other people will think. Fear that God will leave me high and dry. Fear of rejection.

So instead of showing up, I choose to hide. My trust in God hides. I begin seeking something other than God first. This single decision causes ripples that push my faith into hiding. Love is diminished, the image of God within me is squelched, and the invitational life is silenced.

This is the kind of faith story that doesn't end well. It tends to be gripped by fear, laced with severe trust issues, and intent on preserving self at all costs. Then the book of Acts introduces another Ananias. When a vision awakened him and he was called by name, Ananias gave a simple response: "Yes, Lord" (9:10). God gave him instructions to go to a house in Damascus, where there was a man from Tarsus named Saul. Saul was praying and awaiting someone to come and pray over him so that his sight might be restored.

Hearing this, Ananias began to negotiate with God, informing him that Saul was a registered radical trying to stop the Christian movement. God heard all this but said, "Go! This man is my chosen instrument to proclaim my name to the Gentiles and their kings and to the people of Israel" (v. 15).

So Ananias obeyed. He actually went! Would you go? Which Ananias are you more like? The one who chose security in self over trust in God? Or the one who chose trust in God over security in self?

Ananias was probably freaking out as he drew nearer to the house where Saul was staying. I imagine him praying for courage as he was about to face a radical who had openly murdered, beaten, and arrested Christ followers. God called Ananias to go to the leading terrorist of his day. As a result of Ananias's trusting and going, God gave us Paul and all of the beautiful stories that followed.

We can't have it both ways. It would be so convenient if we could trust God while also doing our own thing. But we can't be both hiding and seeking at the same time. We can hide as our ancestors did back in the garden, or we can seek as our God did—and we can relate to him and other people in a much more fulfilling way.

There are stories of pain, sorrow, heartache, addiction, and shame all around us. They are hiding in the hearts of people we pass every day. I have to imagine that if Jesus were to encounter these people, he would earnestly seek relationship in a desire to free them. We get to do that as well. We get to be seekers, actively pursuing those around us who desperately need healing and hope.

One way we can seek others is by asking questions and listening. We can show curiosity about their lives. When we engage and relate to them, they'll think we're awesome. And we'll feel awesome, because contributing to someone else is an invigorating experience. How do we get curious? We open ourselves up to the possibility of being surprised. We leave room for a person to be different from we what assumed.

When you meet someone for the first time, don't assume you know anything about that person. Instead, ask questions. Think about what you really would love to know, and find a way to ask about it.

I met a young woman recently who was studying to be a history teacher. When I asked her what drew her to that field, she said she ultimately hopes to travel to Tibet and serve as a missionary there. From there I asked more about her heart for Tibet. What was it about the place that was so intriguing for her? How did she know that was where she wanted to end up? What was she most excited about and nervous about? I was genuinely curious, and I believe she felt cared about because of my interest.

Some people don't like being asked questions because they feel as if they're being interrogated. Others are just very private and interpret questions as nosiness or excessive familiarity, even if the motive is genuine. This is why we must always invite the Holy Spirit to whisper to us as we connect with others. We must practice discernment and commit to being sensitive to the needs of the other person. With any people we meet, the list of questions is endless once we set aside our assumptions and seek to learn all about them. As they share, we get a glimpse into how God loves them and the many threads of grace that are woven throughout their experiences.

When my wife and I began telling others that we hoped to adopt a child from overseas, we got all sorts of questions. Some were well meaning, some were pointed, and some were clearly based on thinly veiled assumptions. The best and most helpful conversations we had during that time were the ones that began with people saying, "I would love to hear more about your adoption journey. Can you tell me what it's been like so far?" Open-ended questions like this show that the people asking aren't coming with an agenda. They are truly curious and interested. Assured of that, we feel the safety to share from an authentic place.

SOCIAL CHOICES

My wife and I make a habit of walking to our neighborhood park with our two children as often as we can. Usually we'll spend a few minutes pushing the kids on the swings or playing a game of tag. They love this time (and so do we), but it's especially wonderful if we come to the park when other children are there. Within seconds the kids who were strangers just moments before become engaged in some imaginary game together. This leaves us parents with a chance to find a bench and enjoy a few minutes of uninterrupted conversation.

During these times I'm always amazed at children's uncanny ability to instantly make friends. This seems to come naturally for kids, but it doesn't seem to come as naturally for adults. Somewhere along the line of growing up, we stop seeing each other as potential friends and instead start noticing the differences that keep us apart. We become aware of social ladders and receive the message that there are the people you want to be seen with and those you don't.

Why does our natural curiosity wane as we mature? There are a few possible reasons. According to Dr. Stephanie Carlson, an expert on childhood brain development at the University of Minnesota, "Simple lack of practice is one reason."[1] As we're forced to turn our attention to logic, reason, and facts in school, we spend more of our time and brainpower in reality—and less in imagination. We look at what is, not at what can be.

As adults we also suffer from a fear of being wrong. We quickly learn that being wrong often has negative consequences. At school we're penalized for being wrong. At work we're penalized for being wrong. But kids don't worry about that. Willing to be wrong, they bravely forge into new territory. According to Sir Ken Robinson, an expert in creativity, "If you're not prepared to be wrong, you'll never come up with anything original."[2]

So some of us have lost our imaginations. We haven't been practicing the art of potential. Instead, we receive the message projected to us: that the other person is too reckless, arrogant, opinionated, or dogmatic. We settle for that and believe it's all there is to the story. If the story arc of the Bible teaches us anything, it's that there is *always* more to the story. There is always more happening beyond the first impression. We've just forgotten how to imagine it.

Others of us are comfortable with pushing our social boundaries, but we just aren't sure how to do it. We don't want to be pushy or awkward or come across too intense. We want to be able to be normal, to be ourselves, without overthinking it and making it weird. In an effort not to alienate ourselves, we end up caring more about what is right than about engaging in the messy kingdom work of what can be.

The key here is curiosity. Kids are naturally curious. They're actively engaged with their environments 100 percent of the time. They don't assume they know everything about everything. Every experience is viewed as a chance to learn something new—about the world, about God, about one another. Being wrong isn't on their radar, because *everything* is a possibility. Can you imagine for a moment how a perspective like that could change the way you relate to people you might otherwise avoid?

Jesus wasn't the least bit concerned with the way others perceived his social choices. He was constantly putting himself in questionable or uncool or "wrong" social circles. Why? Because he was curious about people. He practiced the discipline of seeing past all the external labels. When society labeled a woman a whore, Jesus saw her as a daughter of the King. When his own disciples scowled at the tax collectors, Jesus saw broken stories and lonely people. Jesus always saw the person, not the label.

Perhaps a childlike faith is a curious faith. How would that apply to the way you're living out your faith now? What would need to change for you to get more curious about the people in your life? Can you commit to being curious about the stories of those you meet? Can you commit to putting God's character of grace on display? If you answered yes, you're well on your way to living the invitational life.

10
FIRST THINGS FIRST

In 2015 I had the privilege of attending the National Prayer Breakfast in Washington, DC. The breakfast has happened the first Thursday in February every year for the past sixty-two years. World leaders convene to hear the president speak, and about three thousand people attend the event.

The House of Representatives organizes the prayer breakfast one year, and the Senate organizes it the next year. A Republican and a Democrat from the House co-chaired the event I attended. This was an especially politically charged pairing, since these two had been going at each other via media and news outlets.

It was ironic to see them standing side by side at the podium, welcoming attendees to the breakfast. I remember one of them saying,

> Welcome to the National Prayer Breakfast. You probably don't believe that this is real between the two of us. Let me just say that for the last

two years, every Wednesday morning for an hour, the two of us and about twenty others from the House gather to pray for one another. We pray for each other's families. We pray for our country and our world.

It's hard to imagine that such fierce opponents could find any common ground. It's hard to believe they would get together to pray in the spirit of peace. How is this possible? How is it that we can find things that unite us and yet at the same time have so many differences?

HOW BELIEFS ARE BORN

There's such a spectrum of meaning in the word *believe*. It can be confusing to know exactly what constitutes a belief compared with an opinion. The word *belief* can be broken down into three categories, which are synonyms for how we talk about what we believe. The first category is *essentials*. When I say essentials, I'm talking about matters of first importance. *What is the most important thing?* As you think of yourself as a Christ follower, what is a matter of first importance? You probably have responses that come to mind quite easily.

When we talk about belief, we're also talking about *convictions*. These are the strong beliefs we hold. People are expressing a conviction when they say something like, "I believe we should be engaged in ending human trafficking." A conviction is based on our understanding and interpretation of Scripture, our internal wiring, and our role as image bearers of God. It is also filtered through our own experiences, pain, and personal stories. Those factors give us convictions or strong beliefs when it comes to how we, as Christ followers, ought to live.

The third category pertaining to belief is *preferences*. This means we give an advantage to one thing over another. We prefer one thing over another thing.

We all have preferences. We all have convictions. We all have essentials. The question is, what holds us together? The Bible has a few things to say about this concept. For instance, throughout the book of 1 Corinthians, Paul referred to convictions, preferences, and essentials. At one point he said, "No one can lay any foundation other than the one already laid, which is Jesus Christ" (3:11). For Paul, Jesus was the foundation. If you ever have the chance to watch builders work, you'll notice that they always start with leveling the land to make sure the foundation is laid properly.

Jesus is the essential foundation. Convictions are the solid footing, the firm base. Preferences are the style we want for the house—the Cape Cod or Victorian style, the wraparound porch, the color of the curtains. The Corinthian church was wrestling through what to do with differing preferences and looked to Paul to help them sort it out. The apostle told them, "My brothers and sisters, some from Chloe's household have informed me that there are quarrels among you. What I mean is this: One of you says, 'I follow Paul'; another, 'I follow Apollos'; another, 'I follow Cephas'; still another, 'I follow Christ'" (1:11–12).

This church experienced division over its leaders and teachers. Some were saying, "I want to follow the apostle, the leader, the builder, or the one who planted this church." Disputes and disunity emerged because people wanted to follow different people. I imagine Paul said, "Hold on! Do you understand the preferences you have? Every one of us brings preferences to the table." As the book progresses, we see that lawsuits eventually broke out within the church. Paul began to ask, "What's going on? You've got lawsuits? You're going to drag each other into a courtroom? You're going to bring your issues to a judge who doesn't follow Christ, who isn't part of our church? This is the way you want to represent Jesus?" (see 6:1–6).

Paul was looking at these believers and asking, "Can't you find someone within the church who can mediate this problem?" And "Is it possible that there is nobody among you wise enough to judge a dispute between believers? But instead, one brother takes another to court—and this in front of unbelievers!" (vv. 5–6).

Paul held a conviction about how the church should represent Jesus, and this bickering behavior over trivial things was certainly out of bounds for him. In 1 Corinthians 15, Paul laid out what he believed was most essential:

> Now, brothers and sisters, I want to remind you of the gospel I preached to you, which you received and on which you have taken your stand. By this gospel you are saved, if you hold firmly to the word I preached to you. Otherwise, you have believed in vain.
>
> For what I received I passed on to you as of first importance. (vv. 1–3)

Paul then unpacked the essentials: the gospel, the good news, the way he started that church, what he preached on, what everyone took their stand on. He reminded the church that Christ died for their sins, was buried, was "raised on the third day according to the Scriptures." He appeared to Cephas and then to the twelve disciples. The risen Christ appeared to five hundred people, to James and the other apostles, and then to Paul (see vv. 1–8).

Paul was saying, "You want to know what's essential? You want to know what is of first importance? It's that Jesus died and rose again. Jesus sat at the right hand of the Father. God looked down on his creation with a plan for redemption. He sent his Son to walk this earth, to enter the brokenness and show people how to walk in harmony with the Father. Jesus taught people about the kingdom of God and how they could have access to the Father. He did so right up to the moment he died. It wasn't just any death—it was sacrificial. He died for everything you've done to God. He died for every wrong you've done to yourself, for every wrong you've done to others, and every wrong you've done to this world. He died for every wrong that has been done to you. He died so that you might live."

On that third day, the resurrection happened. Jesus rose. Death did not have the last word. Death did not win. God's grace brought peace and power that raised Jesus from the dead. Then Jesus made himself known. He appeared to Cephas (Peter). He appeared to the twelve disciples. He appeared to five hundred people. They touched him. They saw him. He told them that God had a plan. He called them and sent them out into the world to be redeemers and restorers of God's intent for this world. Then Jesus ascended back to heaven.

We end up making a mess when we elevate our convictions and our preferences by adding to God's story. One of my mentors says it's as if we're saying our faith is "Jesus plus something." Jesus is the very essence of our faith. His life, death, and resurrection are the foundation. The essentials are all we need to stand on. This is who we are as Jesus followers. We are about Jesus. But things can get tricky because these three categories can feel similar. The essentials are not meant to diminish convictions or preferences, but they are the most important part of our faith. They are the nonnegotiables.

The truth is, my convictions can't save me from my brokenness, but they can lead me to the essentials—to Jesus. My preferences aren't going to redeem me in front of the Father. Only the essentials can do that. On these we build our house, our faith, our lives. This is good news. Out of this truth we're given the energy and passion we need to develop wisdom in our convictions and preferences. It's not about who teaches. It's not about who leads worship. It's not about how we vote. It's not about where we attend church or whether we speak in tongues or not. It's not about any of those things. Those things pale in comparison to being a community solely wrapped around the glory and majesty of Jesus Christ. That's who we are. That's who we will be.

We've got to imagine, though, that as a diverse global faith community of Christians, we are going to have different convictions and preferences. So how do we get along? And how do we relate to those outside Christianity? If we're guided by our convictions and preferences, we won't be effective in showing the world who Jesus is.

We can't expect the world to accept the invitation when we're all over the board with our preferences and convictions. However, people will show up in droves when they see how unmovable we are about Jesus being number one. Consistency and unity are what is needed. As Christians, we need to work to be united in the essentials. Without that, we're just a collection of folks with radically varying opinions.

SEEKING BALANCE

How do we live with the essentials grounding us while also maintaining respect for those who are different from us? Can we engage with someone who votes differently, worships differently, or thinks differently? How do we handle that?

This is exactly the situation Paul saw taking place in Rome. A number of Jews had customs, history, and traditions that were meaningful to them before they found Jesus. A number of Gentiles had come from religions that encouraged idol worship before they found Jesus. These diverse people were united in Jesus. Yet when they gathered together, their cultural backgrounds were at odds with one another. Still, these Christ followers earnestly tried to figure out how to make it work and be the church together.

Similar things happen to us. The personal faith stories we hold are incredibly moving and deep, and they bring so much to the greater Christian community. So how do we live in harmony and show the world we are one body, even when there are differences in our convictions and preferences?

Every one of us is wired uniquely and differently in the image of God. Every one of us has a different type of story. Every one of us has something to offer this world. But many of us look for communities that act like us, look like us, believe like us, and vote like us. Therefore, we insulate ourselves from diversity in the church. And worse, we're so sequestered that we don't relate to people outside the church.

What we know of heaven is that every tongue, tribe, and nation will come together (see Rev. 7:9). Heaven is going to be a global cultural party of rich diversity. All of God's creation will be united because we've experienced the essence of faith in Christ: Jesus walking and teaching and dying and being buried. We've experienced the poured-out blood for our sins. We've experienced the salvation that comes from Jesus's sacrifice on the cross.

In Romans 14 and 15, Paul was saying that there are some people whose faith is weak and some people whose faith is strong. People who are weak in their faith don't yet have the conscious awareness of freedom that is found in Christ and Christ alone. They're easily swayed by preferences and convictions. The unwavering believers, the ones who know freedom in Christ, are saying, "You can engage in this activity. Why don't you do this? You have freedom—you can do this." While they are perhaps trying to encourage those weaker in the faith, what they are in fact doing is pushing them to a place of shame and embarrassment. They effectively create obstacles to the experience of grace and peace.

Paul said this is not okay. He told the strong to accept and welcome those who were at different places in their faith. He admonished them not to get caught up having useless conversations over disputable matters. Basically, he said it's not worth arguing over preferences and convictions.

The topic of parenting comes to mind. We have to navigate issues in our modern world that aren't specifically addressed in the Scriptures. For instance, how many hours should our kids spend on the Internet? At what age should we allow them to have cell phones? What type of music is appropriate for our teenagers? What is an appropriate curfew? As parents we all have ideas, preferences, and convictions. It's so easy for us to offer advice: "You know, you should do it *this* way." We mean well, but advice usually doesn't help. The reality is, there are countless ways to parent. We agree that our essential job as parents is to love, nurture, and provide for our children, but how we all get there may look very different.

You might have a particular conviction. You might have a particular preference. And that's between you and God. Live out those convictions and preferences in a way that honors God. Someone sitting beside you, behind you, or in front of you might have an opposing conviction or preference. You know what that person's responsibility is? To honor God. To live in a way that brings glory to God. Paul was saying this is not about division. The church has to be united, and what unites us are the essentials.

There can be diversity with regard to convictions and preferences, and the ways we navigate them as believers is crucial to us as the church. Paul said in Romans 14:13, "Let us stop passing judgment on one another. Instead, make up your mind not to put any stumbling block or obstacle in the way of a brother or sister." We don't want any barrier that's going to push people away from having their hands open and their hearts fully surrendered to God. Make up your mind to be a Christian who focuses on Jesus and the essentials. Let's be careful not to be people who create barriers and stumbling blocks for others who are in different places spiritually than we are.

Paul admonished those who were strong in their faith to be patient and kind to those who were weaker in the faith. He specifically warned against pointing out every failing as a way to elevate our own pride. Basically, Paul was saying, quit trying to be right about every little thing.

Recently I was walking through the aisles of my local market when I heard someone talking about God. I was getting so upset internally because he just wasn't doing it right. He was saying things all wrong. I found myself wanting to correct his preferences, point out where he was wrong, and show him why I was right. I wanted to engage with him, not to develop a deeper faith or to encourage him, but to prove I was right. What was I thinking?

That's not the gospel at all. The gospel is this, as Paul said in Romans 15:7: "Accept one another, then, just as Christ accepted you, in order to bring praise to God." Accepting one another in your home, church, and community is an act of worship to God. If someone has a different conviction or preference than you and you can't accept that person, then you aren't bringing praise and worship to God. What you're saying is, "God, you accepted me, but I'm not accepting anybody else. God, you accepted me and I know you accepted them, but I'm not accepting them." Paul reminds us that God has accepted us, and the invitation is to accept others, no matter where they are on the spiritual continuum.

People who understand the essentials and go deep with Jesus will naturally orient their lives around loving Christ, following Christ, and imitating Christ. A Christ-centered, Christlike life is certainly compelling. It bears the kind of fruit people want to taste and see. It draws people in.

Let's make a big deal about the essentials, not our convictions or preferences. That's how we can engage and relate with people, and that's how their hearts will soften toward our invitation. We need to give up judging nonbelievers. Our judgments of them keep us from sharing the essentials. We might catch ourselves thinking, *They wouldn't want to hear about Jesus.... They would never accept an invitation to come to church.... They're so lost, they'll never hear the gospel.* Don't assume anything, but instead ask questions, listen well, and remain curious.

If someone were to ask me, "Steve, why are you here? Why are you a Christian?" I'd say I'm here because of two high school students, Dominic and Nathan (the guys I mentioned in chapter 8). Dominic came up to me and said out of the blue, "Do you want to know how to dominate life?" These two guys taught me the essentials and completely changed the trajectory of my life. I didn't know convictions. I didn't know preferences. I didn't know any of that stuff. But I understood the essentials, and those are what changed my life.

What would you say if someone were to ask you why you're here, why you are walking this earth, what your purpose is, and what you believe in? If you understand the essentials, then the answer is you know that God has a plan for you. He's crazy about you. He sent his Son for you. He wants to redeem you and restore you. God's inviting you to believe that you have a purpose. You have a meaning. You have something to offer the kingdom of God. Jesus plus nothing has the power to change everything.

PART IV

RISK

11
"HELP!"

To celebrate ten years of marriage, my wife and I planned a vacation to Hawaii. We saved up for months as we dreamed and prepped for the trip.

Our condo was set upon a rocky coastline overlooking the ocean, presenting us with daily humpback-whale sightings and more turtles than we could count. We'd wake to the crashing waves and toast to breathtaking sunsets every evening. It was one of those "once in a lifetime" trips, and we soaked in every second of it.

One afternoon while we were out on the patio grilling fish freshly caught that day, happily watching whales breach as the sun began to set, I suddenly heard someone scream, "Help!"

I ran to the edge of the cliff overlooking a cove. The tides were changing from low to high as evidenced by a set of seven-foot waves crashing toward the shore. A woman's arms reached out from the foamy water. It was as though she was attempting to climb a wall but couldn't find her grip.

Every day the tides changed in this little cove. When it was low tide, the water was shallow enough to stand and float among the sea life swirling underneath. But when a sea change occurred, the tides would rise and bigger wave sets came barreling in, transforming what was once a tranquil little cove into something much more dangerous.

The woman's head popped out of the water, and again she screamed, "Help!" Another set of waves was rolling in, so I started to run. I ran past the rows of condominiums and beach shacks, leaping over volcanic rock and pathways as I sprinted to the shore.

Growing up in California, I had a friend who had devoted his life to becoming a lifeguard. As I was running, my heart beating so hard I thought it might leap right out of my chest, all I could think about were his words, the same words he'd say quietly to himself before he took his post: "Not on my watch!" No one was going to die on his watch.

As I dove into the water, I kept praying, *Not on my watch. Not on my watch.* I took a few huge dives under the crashing waves and worked hard to keep the woman in my sights as I swam closer. When I finally reached her, she was struggling badly, barely able to breathe and turning a faint shade of blue. Instinct kicked in as I put her on my back and began paddling as fast as I could to shore. I carried her to the sand, laid her down, and begged her to live.

Within seconds her two kids, who had been watching desperately from the shore, ran up to her with tears in their eyes. She was shaking from the shock, but with some air in her lungs, she got her bearings and sat up. She reached hungrily for her kids and drew them into her arms. As she held them, she turned to me and whispered a small but emphatic "Thank you."

Breathless and incredibly grateful, I began to walk back to my condo. As I stepped over the rocks lining the shore, I looked up at the cliff and saw at least fifty people standing and watching what had just transpired. Immediately God spoke to me and said, "How often have you stood on a cliff and watched someone drown?"

Names started coming to mind from my past and present of people who were drowning in

- Addictions
- Troubled marriages
- Financial problems
- Grief
- Doubt
- Deep struggles with faith

As I walked back to the condo, people gave me high fives, congratulating me on my bravery. Yet with tears in my eyes, all I could think about were the hundreds of times I had watched people drown whom I professed to care for. For the rest of my time on the island, I couldn't shake seeing myself as one of the people standing on the cliff, arms crossed, while people around me were crying out for help.

The image was haunting, and one question in particular convicted my spirit: Why was I so willing to drop everything and risk my life to rescue a stranger and yet claim to be too busy to care for those in my life whom I know need rescuing? What was keeping me from risking for their sakes?

SAFETY FIRST

I grew up in a small suburban town that was committed to being the safest city in California. Blue-ribbon schools, clean streets, no graffiti, and minimal crime were staples of our community. I learned to avoid "problem areas" and "those people" who were different from me. Early in my life, through words and actions, I was trained what to see and what not to see. Part of my upbringing was steeped in the avoidance of struggle, pain, and discomfort.

My grandfather was a four-star general. During World War II, the phrase *calculated risk* began to circulate throughout the military. Generals would calculate the risk of how many B-24 bombers they would lose if they attempted a proposed mission. Once hypothetical possibilities and outcomes were discussed among the leadership, the highest in command would determine whether the potential casualties were worth the attempt.

The phrase *calculated risk* later became prominent in business and human-resource circles. The thought went something like this: We're interested in hiring person A. We recognize that she doesn't have the experience, but she has the natural instincts, and we think she'll thrive with the right coaching. So a risk is calculated, and if the potential value gained outweighs the cost to reach it, we move forward. We make the leap. We take the risk.

In universities all across the country, courses are based on the idea of risk management. Every great leader understands the expectation to identify and manage potential threats and dangers to an organization.

All of that is fine and good, but what happens when our gospel becomes a matter of risk management? What happens when our churches find themselves constantly calculating risks? What happens when Christ followers become averse to risk? What happens when the church is okay with standing on a cliff and watching?

Unfortunately, within our modern society, a subtle message of "safety above all" has been perpetuated. We pray for safety. We tell our children to be safe, and we use the adage "safety first." Pain is a terrifying subject that we go to great measures to avoid. Our mantra is "Shield yourself from all forms of risk, and risk only if there is a good chance the calculations will come out in your favor. Don't step out. Don't fail. Don't put yourself in danger. Don't be fully seen. Don't risk."

A pain-free life sounds nice, doesn't it? The problem is, I don't see this message anywhere in the New Testament. A life based on the gospel of safety is sure to be a long and boring one. Life happens in the mess; character is built during struggle. We get knocked down only to discover the strength we have to rise again. All throughout the New Testament, we see people compelled by love and grace to risk it all and proclaim with their one and only life, "Not on my watch."

I want this same kind of life for you and for me. But how do we get it? It starts with some plants.

BREATH OF LIFE

In the 1700s, Dutch scientist Jan Ingenhousz discovered the reason a plant raised inside was more likely to die than one raised outside. The primary belief at that time was that if you had adequate soil, water, and strong roots, vegetation would grow. Ingenhousz discovered there was more to the story. He came to realize that you needed the sun and breath as well as water, soil, and roots for plant life to grow. It was this scientist who discovered the process of photosynthesis, which means "from the light."

Ingenhousz realized that

- the sun gives off light;
- light is a form of energy; and
- the leaves from the tree capture that energy.

Water is made up of two atoms of hydrogen and one atom of oxygen. The energy these leaves capture from the sun splits up the hydrogen and the oxygen. The plants release the oxygen to us, and in return they take in our exhaled breath of carbon dioxide (CO_2). Our CO_2 mixes with the two atoms of hydrogen to create a sugary substance called glucose, which feeds the trees. Just by breathing, you are giving life to nature.

If you're like me, you don't wake up trying to bring your A game to breathing. It's not as if I walk up to a tree, breathe on it, and say, "Here you go, buddy." God wired us from the very beginning to give life, whether we're aware of it or not. God's intent was that we wouldn't be passive participants in giving life, but that it would be at the forefront of everything we do. It's in giving life that we receive life.

To take this even further, rabbis for years have wrestled over the name of God. The Hebrew alphabet is made up of twenty-two letters. There are no vowels, and three of the twenty-two letters are silent. The three silent letters make up the name Yahweh (*yod, hey, vov*). Rabbis began to wonder, *Why would God refer to himself with a name filled with silent letters?* They realized that the letters weren't actually silent; they were the sounds of inhaling and exhaling—the "sound of breathing."[1] So every time you breathe, you're not just giving life to nature; you're also saying the letters that make up the holiest name.

By just breathing, you're giving life and praising God, whether you know it or not. Or maybe better said, whether you choose it or not.

From the beginning, from our days in the garden, the invitation has been for us to live in congruence with how we were wired. In Deuteronomy 30, Moses was preparing the Hebrew people to enter the Promised Land. He had some instructions for how Yahweh wanted the people to live, so Moses stood before them and said, "This day I call the heavens and the earth as witnesses against you that I set before you life and death, blessings and curses. Now choose life" (v. 19).

Moses understood the difference between God and all the other counterfeit gods the Hebrew people would encounter. Moses knew that God decided to allow his glory and image to rest not in some idol crafted by human hands but rather in humanity itself. God entrusted his story, his ways, and his identity to us. We are to showcase to the world what God is actually like. Moses was reminding the people of this saying: "Life and death, blessings and curses are all around you. It's your choice. Now. Choose. Life."

The word *choose* in Hebrew is *bahar*, and it implies that "what you choose you boldly proclaim is the best possible way to live." Every choice you make matters because it proclaims what you think is best and what you believe God is truly like.

In the late 1990s, Dr. Dre discovered a hip-hop artist in a freestyle battle. The kid was from Detroit, Michigan, and had a brashness, raw energy, and quick wit that impressed Dre. In the world of hip-hop, many artists have multiple names for themselves, but this kid had three alternate personalities. One was cynical, one bitter, and the other more hopeful. Dr. Dre and Interscope Records signed Eminem and helped him release his album *The Slim Shady LP*. This album introduced the world to a sarcastic, cocky, throw-anyone-under-the-bus alter ego that shouted the things people thought but would never say. It took the world by storm.

Fifteen months later, Eminem released *The Marshall Mathers LP*, which took a decidedly different turn. This album detailed the pain and brokenness in his life as he aired his past and all the dirty laundry it entailed. He rapped openly about addiction, about his mother, and about his ex-wife. Yet still there was no movement toward health and reconciliation; this was essentially tell-it-like-it-is verbal vomit from his perspective. Suburbia ate it up, buying almost two million copies in the first week the album dropped.

Then he released *The Eminem Show*. At this point he had our attention and even our sympathy. These lyrics weren't angry; they weren't the words of a victim. They were hopeful, strong, and confident. Song after song expressed the thoughts of a person who, no matter what anyone said, was going to live his one and only life to the fullest.

We all have similar personalities within us, don't we? Someone says something cutting or harsh, and we want to respond with sarcasm and judgment. Someone does something cruel, and we react with bitterness. I know I'm guilty of this. But then there are days when I'll risk it all, overwhelmed by a hope and belief that rescue is possible.

Who in your life is screaming for help? How are you participating in the active contribution to life around you? What do your daily choices say about what you believe about God? Moses said every choice matters. The danger of free will is that each one of us has the opportunity to choose safety, comfort, bitterness, and even death instead of life. Moses knew the kind of violation these choices would bring. He warned us that a life lived apart from hope, faith, and risk leads to spiritual death. More than our own death, it eliminates the potential witness we hold to bear God's true nature to those who don't yet know him.

So what do our lives proclaim about God when we stand on a cliff and watch people drown every day? That God wouldn't risk it all for them? That God wouldn't care to engage in that conflict? Or that God wouldn't want to rescue and redeem that situation?

The invitation to life that God extended to the Hebrew people is available to us today. The opportunity to choose life doesn't expire. Today, even now, we have the chance to align our lives with the way God's heart beats for humanity. We are hardwired to give life and to choose life, to continuously choose to declare what God is all about. We get to be givers and guardians of life. They will know we are Christians by our love (see John 13:35). What makes us different is that instead of going with the flow and avoiding pain as much as possible, we are the ones who dive headfirst into the pain, into the stories, of those in our lives. As Christians we won't stand on the cliffs with our arms crossed, watching humanity drown. It's only by risking it all that we'll discover what God is truly like.

12
ENGAGE THE DISRUPTION

Jesus often fielded attacks and accusations that were disguised as innocent questions. Many people—religious people, actually—were less than thrilled with the ways Jesus challenged their system. He made them uncomfortable, and his perspective of faith was convicting to those who had forgotten the God they professed to serve. As Luke 10:25 says, "On one occasion an expert in the Law stood up to test Jesus. 'Teacher,' he asked, 'what must I do to inherit eternal life?'"

This may seem like a softball question for a teacher like Jesus. He could talk about heaven. He could talk about life after death. He could talk about eternity with God. However, this wasn't what the expert in the law was asking. In the Jewish context, when you heard the phrase *eternal life*, it meant simply, "How do I live with God now? How do I live in step, in tune, in harmony with the almighty God today? How do I live a life with sincere significance and meaning in the here and now?"

This expert in the Law stood up and put Jesus on the witness stand, instantly causing everyone around them to become the jury.

They were all looking at Jesus. How would he respond? "Tell us, teacher, what must we do to inherit eternal life?"

Jesus brilliantly answered with a question to elevate the conversation to one about the heart rather than the mind. He was helping the person asking the question discover what he already believed to be true.

We can do this too. Often when we try to share information about Jesus, God, or the Bible, people start asking questions. This might put us on the defensive. But if we ask questions and keep probing into another person's life, we not only control the conversation, but we also create an opening for the gospel to be shared more effectively than if we go around spewing truths at people.

We all have things we need to relearn and unlearn about God. Spending time with Jesus will expose those areas in us.

So Jesus responded, "What is written in the Law? ... How do you read it?" (v. 26). Essentially he was saying, "You're the expert in the Law, and you're asking me? Tell me what's written in the Law as you understand it."

The Law in the Jewish mind was the Torah, the first five books of the Bible: Genesis, Exodus, Leviticus, Numbers, and Deuteronomy. Within these five books are 613 commandments, known in Hebrew as *mitzvot*. To the Hebrew people, they weren't laws and commands; they were sacred deeds. They were ways for people to walk in step and in tune with God. Rabbis agreed that the most important command was to "love the LORD your God with all your heart and with all your soul and with all your strength" (Deut. 6:5).

There was great debate, however, over what should be considered the second greatest commandment. Fifty years before the days of Jesus, two rabbis, Rabbi Hillel and Rabbi Shammai, had public debates over this topic. The gospel writers showcased eight of these debates. According to Hillel, the two greatest commandments were to "love the Lord your God with all your heart and with all your soul and with all your strength and with all your mind," and to "love your neighbor as yourself" (Luke 10:27). But Shammai was a literalist. He said, "No, no, no—the first commandment is to love the Lord your God with all your heart, with all your soul, and with all your mind; the second greatest commandment is to be holy, as God is holy."

So when Jesus turned the expert's question back to him, he was asking the man to show his cards and the theology he followed. Jesus essentially said, "Hey, expert of the Law, since you know the Law, how do you interpret it? Whom do you follow?" Look what the man said: "'Love the Lord your God with all your heart and with all your soul and with all your strength and with all your mind'; and 'Love your neighbor as yourself'" (v. 27).

Jesus quickly responded. "You have answered correctly.... Do this and you will live" (v. 28). Basically he was saying, "You got it. If you want to know how to inherit eternal life, love God and love your neighbor as yourself. Do this and you will live the full, good life."

While you would think that hearing this from Jesus would clear up the matter, the expert still wanted Jesus to be on the stand. He looked at Jesus and said, "Who is my neighbor?" (v. 29). It's a great question. In those days, a neighbor was defined by the word *rea*, which in Hebrew refers to someone close by, someone from your own tribe, and maybe even someone from your own country. It definitely didn't mean the pagans, the Gentiles, or the Samaritans. A neighbor was someone from the same tribe. Neighbors looked, dressed, ate, behaved, and believed the same.

This expert in the Law was trying to box Jesus in by asking him a pointed question. Who do you say a neighbor is? So Jesus told a story. He answered with a parable.

Before we look at Jesus's words, I want to take you to the ancient Near East and paint a picture of how this audience would have heard the parable. This has great implications for us today, so let's pretend we're gathered around Jesus, listening to the story for the first time.

A man was going down from Jerusalem to Jericho when robbers attacked him. They stripped him of his clothes, beat him, and went away, leaving him half dead (see v. 30). We don't know where this man was from; all we know is that he was headed from Jerusalem to Jericho.

Scholars say that this road was one of the most dangerous places to travel in the ancient Near East. It winds and curves so that you can't see what is around the bend ahead of you. So Jesus tells us that attackers blindsided this man and violently beat, stripped, and robbed him, leaving him half dead on the trail.

Back then, the two easiest ways to identify where someone originated were by clothing and speech. This man was naked and unconscious, making it impossible to know where he was from. We don't know whether he was a Jew; we don't know if he was an enemy. Without any identification, the man in Jesus's story was really just a man. No context—all we know is that he was lying there about to die.

Jesus said, "A priest happened to be going down the same road, and when he saw the man, he passed by on the other side" (v. 31). A priest was part of the upper class, and many scholars believe that the majority of priests lived in the city of Jericho. Priests would take shifts working alongside Levites and religious laypeople in the temple, two weeks on and two weeks off. Picture this priest: an upper-class man returning home after two weeks of rigorous work.

The priest saw this man ... and decided to keep going. Why would he do that?

Forget what we've been taught about being in a hurry. This wasn't a time-management issue. It was about how the priest ranked the Law, how he understood the Torah, and which rabbinic theology he followed. Did he believe the second greatest commandment was to love his neighbor or to remain holy?

If this priest stopped to help this man and came in contact with his wounds, he would have become ceremonially unclean. He would have had to return to the temple and enter into a ritual of cleansing that often included public shaming. People would have said, "Oh, you can't do your job. You couldn't stay holy."

This priest had to make a decision: *Is this person worth the shame I will endure? Is this person worth the mocking I will endure? Is this person worth my having to go back to Jerusalem and be unclean? Is this person worth it?* No. This man wasn't worth it to the priest. Holiness was the value he held.

The second character we meet in Jesus's story was a Levite. The Levites handled security at the temple. They managed the grounds and maintained order, and they too would head home at the end of working two weeks. They were not upper class, so the Levite probably was walking, not riding on a horse. His boss, the priest, had already left for home, and now here the Levite was on the same trail.

When the Levite came to where the beaten man was lying, he faced a choice. How did he rank the Law? Love God, love your neighbor? Love God, be holy? What did his boss, the priest, do? His boss passed by this man. The Levite might have thought, *If I don't do the same, what am I saying about my boss? I can't disrespect him.*

The priest passed by, and so did the Levite. Since this was a very narrow road, it's not as if there was a lot of space to pass by the man in need. It's more like they had to step over him. The priest stepped over him. The Levite stepped over him.

If you had been listening to Jesus tell the story, you would have anticipated the progression of characters he was building toward. Describing the hierarchy of the temple, Jesus had introduced a priest and a Levite, and the next character would presumably be a religious layperson, who would also have been on his way home after serving in the temple.

Jesus, however, introduced a character that no one saw coming—a Samaritan. Using that word at the time was like using a racist, derogatory term.

Jesus said, "But a Samaritan, as he traveled, came where the man was; and when he saw him, he took pity on him" (v. 33).

The priest saw the wounded man and just kept going. The Levite came to the place, saw the man, and kept walking. But the Samaritan came to the place, saw him, and had pity on him. The word *pity* is my favorite word in Greek. It's the word *splagchnon*, which means "compassion from your bowels." It's used eleven times in the New Testament.

But here's the idea: This man, this Samaritan, saw the guy lying there, nearly dead, beaten. But he didn't just notice him; he had compassion on him. This wasn't compassion that says, "Oh, I feel bad for you." It was compassion that says, "I have to do something about this."

The scripture says he went to the man and bandaged his wounds. He touched the man, getting his hands messy, dirty, and bloody. What's more, he poured oil and wine on the man's wounds. This is what he would have brought to the temple for worship. And now he was pouring it out, trying to heal this man.

Then the Samaritan put the man on his own donkey, which means he walked beside the donkey. The Samaritan made the rest of the journey on foot so that the injured man could be carried. In the Near East, if you walked a donkey or a horse, it was because you were a servant for whoever was riding beside you. The Samaritan brought the man to an inn and took care of him. He sat by his bedside, nursing him, doing what he could to help heal him. Do you understand how brave this Samaritan was?

It's difficult in our day and age to comprehend the risk this Samaritan was taking, but this man put his life on the line. It would have been so easy for someone to take a look at the scene and assume that the Samaritan had been the one who harmed the injured man. It's possible that someone would have accused him, taken him into custody, or taken his life on the spot. Nonetheless, this Samaritan stayed with the man and, when he got up the next morning, left money and asked the innkeeper to look after him. "When I return, I will reimburse you for any extra expense you may have" (v. 35).

Think about the attackers. They robbed the man and beat him nearly to death. They abandoned him and left him to die. The Samaritan came to rescue, heal, and care for the broken man. He then promised that he would return. Does it sound like a familiar story? Does it sound like the gospel?

This is the good news. Isn't this what Jesus did for us? When we were broken and abandoned, Jesus came. When we had no hope for rescue, Jesus came. When we were forgotten, considered unclean, and damaged, Jesus came. He carried us. He stayed with us. He nursed us. He paid for us. He promised to return. The Good Samaritan is a picture of Christ.

But Jesus wasn't finished with the story yet. He had another question for the expert in the Law. He asked, "Which of these three do you think was a neighbor to the man who fell into the hands of robbers?" (v. 36).

When the expert asked the question, he made the word *neighbor* a noun. When Jesus asked the question, he made *neighbor* (or *neighboring*) a verb. The expert in the Law could only answer, "The one who had mercy on him." He couldn't even name the Samaritan. Jesus told the expert, "Go and do likewise" (v. 37).

This isn't a story about random acts of kindness. This is a story about intentional love. This is a story that asks us how far our idea of "neighbor" extends. Is it only the person who lives next door to you—the person who looks like you, votes like you, and acts like you? Or could it be the person you never saw coming?

Jesus was making a declaration that to be his disciple means more than just loving people who are similar or socially acceptable. His disciples will love their enemies. His disciples will love without exception, without qualification, and without question. Welcome to the kingdom of God.

A RADICAL KIND OF LOVE

Will we love our enemies? Maybe you hear that question and think, *I don't have enemies. There isn't anyone I don't like. There's no one I hate. No one in my life causes that kind of discomfort for me.*

If that's true for you, then your life might be too safe. It might be too comfortable. As followers of Jesus, we *should* be rubbing shoulders with people who disagree with us. How else are they ever going to experience the inclusive kingdom of God if we spend our energy avoiding them? They *should* be seeing the way we live and thinking, *That confronts everything about how I live.*

How then do we love our enemies? Jesus would say that even the tax collectors can love those who are like them. It's easy for us to love people who always say yes to us or appreciate us or thank us. Jesus said even the pagans will do that. In order to love our enemies, we first have to name them. Who's your enemy? Name him. The expert in the Law from Jesus's story couldn't even name his enemy. He called him "the one who showed mercy."

Can you name the person who hurt you? Say the name. It's the first step in reconciliation. Maybe you start with the titles you use to reference the person: "My ex. My former boss. That punk." You might even say, "The church hurt me." If we are ever going to love the way Jesus loves, we have to start there.

When we can say our enemies' names, we start to see them as humans, not categories. When we can see them as people, we can move toward prayer on their behalf. Can you pray for the people you can't stand? Maybe the prayer is simply, *God, I don't like them, but I'm willing to be changed.* That's a great start.

Someone once deeply wounded a friend of mine. Afterward, my friend committed to pray and journal about the situation for sixty days. When that prayer time began, it was short, intense, and angry. But sixty days later, the prayers were filled with compassion and a deep desire for healing. Prayer is a powerful tool we can access as we strive toward a more Christlike love. Can you pray for the people who have wronged you?

The two commandments are to love God and to love our neighbor as ourselves. The way we love our neighbor is an extension of how well we love ourselves. If someone has abused or otherwise violated you, it would be unwise to get into that relationship again. However, I'm not talking about those who are dangerous to us; I'm talking about dislikes, preferences, and annoyances that prompt us to put up walls.

We're to engage in the disruption. It's Peacemaking 101. Where there is a disruption, where there is chaos, our job as Christ followers is to bring order. We are disciples who see humanity first, not law. Love God. Love others. Everyone, always. We're asked to engage with the chaos and pain and breakdown in relationships. The priest and Levite decided to ignore the humanity bleeding out in front of them. They did not engage. They didn't work to restore. Restoration won't happen on its own.

Pray that God would give you strength and clarity. Seek to understand. I say this because often our enemies are actually provoking something broken inside us. God is so crazy about you that he wants to heal every part of you, even those broken, fragile parts that perhaps feel threatened by the differences of another. Seek to understand what's going on inside yourself, and get curious about why you're reacting that way. Surrender that to God, admit it, confess it, and let it go.

Likewise, get curious about the stories of those you dislike. When my son began first grade, he had his first encounter with a bully. This kid would relentlessly tease, poke, chase, and bother my son. The first few weeks of school saw lots of tears at bedtime as he would share what was going on. We talked with his teacher, brought her and the school team into the problem, and developed a plan to help improve the situation. We also talked to our son. We gave him tools to manage when he felt trapped or teased by the bully.

We also asked him to get curious. What would make a kid his age act so cruelly? Where was he learning that behavior? It led to a really important conversation about empathy and the plight of many children who don't come from homes where love and security are paramount values. We never said the behavior was okay, and we helped our son learn to stand up for himself and ask for help. But we also took the opportunity to teach compassion and the importance of searching for humanity in the midst of the conflict.

Ultimately the bully tired of singling out my son, and tensions eased up. A few months later, my son told me he'd invited the former bully to join in a game of tag at recess—essentially making a step toward friendship. Today there is peace. His teacher reports there haven't been any more incidents, and my son seems to have moved on too. It may seem insignificant, but I believe that experience greatly impacted his ability to speak up for himself as well as extend empathy.

SEEK TO UNDERSTAND

When we genuinely try to understand the people who have wronged us, our hearts change toward them. We might see that a particular incident is part of a bigger issue. It might be that a bully goes to bed hungry every night, sleeps in dirty sheets, and falls asleep to his parents violently fighting. He could be teased, abused, hit, and shamed at home. So what other sorts of behavior could we possibly expect from him at school?

All convicts, punks, thugs, terrorists, racists, extremists, and fundamentalists have a history and a context that have led to their behavior. It doesn't make what they do okay, but it does change our hearts toward them. It does shine a light on the areas of their lives that are in desperate need of God's love and healing.

This isn't easy work, but it's a chance to go deeper in our discipleship with Jesus. We get to grow in our trust and dependency on him. Life with Christ isn't going to be safe or comfortable, but it is going to be rich and satisfying. We can use controversial, difficult, and uncomfortable situations to share the gospel, to be the hands and feet of Jesus, and to point others toward him. When we find ourselves thinking of a person or a people group as "those people" or applying labels, it can serve as a warning bell to change course internally.

In the Sermon on the Mount, Jesus talked extensively about how imperative it was for his followers to develop control over their thoughts. He identified sin not only in terms of action but also in terms of thought. So the way we think of others directly correlates to our ability to love them as he does.

Jesus gives us two specific ways to develop this sort of compassionate and unconditional love for others. In Matthew 6 he tells us how to give to the poor (vv. 3–4). This is so brilliant, because he is ensuring that we remain humble, that we never forget that everything we have comes from the goodness of God. He makes sure that our lives are actively engaged with those who are struggling and in need. These are people desperate and lonely, unable to care for themselves. Jesus encourages us to be near them. They will remind us that we're all in this earthly struggle together.

Then, Jesus tells us how to pray (vv. 5–8). Of course, he went on to deliver the most exquisite prayer in all of history, so perfect in every word (vv. 9–13). We can be thankful that perfect prayers aren't expected of us. Honesty and humility are all we need to come before the throne of heaven and submit to a change of heart.

So you want to learn how to love without condition? Pray. Talk to God. Ask for forgiveness, guidance, and protection. You want to learn to love? Care for the poor.

This takes discipline and awareness, skills we develop over time as we commit to studying the Word, diving into authentic community, and relating to those who don't yet know Jesus. Maybe it's time to consider a tangible way to engage with the poor in your community. Maybe now is the time to commit to opening your heart in genuine prayer. All of heaven is eager for you to join the work of global redemption.

13
ROOFS AND WELLS

When I was in college, eight friends and I piled into a few cars and drove six hours to a concert venue to see one of our favorite bands perform. When we arrived, the place was jam-packed with people, and we were stuck in the very back, struggling to see the stage. All the excitement leading up to the show had been squelched until my buddy Kipp said, "The only way we can get to the front is if we crawl." So that's what we did. Tommy, Kipp, Troy, and I got on all fours, crawling around like toddlers, and within ten minutes we had made it to the front of the stage.

That kind of urgency plays out in all kinds of ways throughout our lives. It's that itchy, burning determination to reach a goal no matter what. But it's also fueled by a rush to reach that goal as quickly as possible. Does a story come to mind for you? Was there a time when you had such a sense of urgency that you felt nothing could stand in your way?

URGENT FAITH

In the ancient Near East, having a physical ailment of any kind presented all sorts of dangers. You were at the mercy of others to take pity on you and help you with basic needs. In the book of Mark, we meet four guys whose friend was paralyzed. They'd heard the stories of Jesus and the miracles he'd performed, and they were urgently working on a plan.

I imagine it was one of the four friends who said, "You know what? I heard Jesus is here. What if we were to bring our friend to meet him? What might happen?" So they carried their friend to the house where Jesus was staying. There was music, food, celebration, excitement—and so many people crowded inside that the five of them couldn't get in.

One of them said, "Let's get up to the roof." He told the other friends, "You see those ropes—let's make a pulley system. I'll take care of the roof. Meet me up there in ten minutes."

So the one guy went up to the roof and began removing some of the hay and mud. Then he started tearing shingles off the roof. Jesus was inside the house, teaching people. Suddenly dust fell from above. Everyone looked up. And there was a guy being lowered on a wooden pallet.

When Jesus saw the faith of this man's friends, he said to the paralyzed man, "Son, your sins are forgiven" (2:5). When Jesus saw their desperate determination, when he saw their ruthless urgency to help their friend, he spoke forgiveness over him. I think Jesus was being a little bit provocative at this moment, because Pharisees and religious leaders were in the crowd, and they were already looking for a reason to arrest him.

"Who do you think you are?" they asked. "You can forgive sins?"

Jesus replied, "Well, what's easier—forgiving sins or healing a man who's paralyzed?" They began to think about it, and Jesus responded, "I'll heal him anyway." So he said to the man, "Get up, take your mat and go home" (v. 11). And the guy got up and walked.

Everyone in the house was in awe. Lives were changed as the crowd was touched by God's great love. It all started because Jesus saw the faith of four friends.

Do you ever wonder why we don't see miracles like this today? What if we exercised our faith for the people around us—and lives were impacted as a result?

In college I was given a car—a 1982 Ford LTD Country Squire to be exact. They don't make 'em like they used to. Simulated wood paneling outside and faux leather inside. It was fantastic. It had four seats in the front row. It had four seats in the second row. I could even squeeze two more in the very back, where a table popped up with magnetic checkers. This car was legendary!

My faith was fresh and new, and I had a desire to see those in my life find themselves swept up in God's great love like I had been. I thought about ways to reach out, ways to engage, ways to invite people to come and see with me. I started to put a name to every seat in that Country Squire. I thought of Ike on my basketball team. I thought about Jeremy, who worked at Pottery Barn with me. I thought about Rob and Tim, two guys I worked with at a local bar. I imagined a name on every seat, and I prayed over each one daily. I had a determination to reach my friends who were doubting or searching or exploring or wanting nothing to do with God. What if I could bring them with me to church and they could meet Jesus?

What might happen with their lives? What would happen in their families?

So I started concocting a plan. There's a church in downtown Los Angeles that meets at a bar, so I would say to some of my friends, "Hey, let's go to the bar in LA." And I would take them to this church. Then afterward we'd go to a concert or grab some food and hang out. On the drive home I'd ask them questions about faith—what they thought about what they had heard. God did incredible things through those conversations, which led to decisions to follow Christ. I was surprised at how these activities solidified friendships. The consistency developed a deep sense of safety so that I was often the one people called when something hard or tragic happened. During this time I learned what it looked like to offer the ministry of presence.

A few years later I was working as a junior high pastor, ministering to a rowdy and fantastic group of kids in Michigan. One weekend I taught about the four friends in Mark 2. I told my students about the car I drove and about praying over the seats. I challenged those kids, saying, "Do you recognize that the car God gave to your parents is an incredible opportunity for you to take a risk for God's kingdom?"

I encouraged them to pray that God would give them a name of someone they could pray for and possibly invite to church. Two weeks later, while I was waiting for students to arrive for youth group, a 1982 Ford LTD Country Squire wood-paneled station wagon pulled up in front of the church. The driver, the dad of one of my students, walked to the back and opened the tailgate. Kids started piling out. One, two, three, four ... eventually sixteen!

My youth-group student got out last. He looked at me and, in his coolest voice, said, "It's the miracle of the station wagon."

Here's the thing: a few months later, seven of those kids chose to be baptized.

It all started because one junior high student had the determination and urgency to pray over every seat in his dad's station wagon. He began to believe that if his friends had the opportunity to meet Jesus, their lives would be better.

Do you believe that? Do you believe that your friends who are far from God would be better off if Christ was at the center of their lives? If so, what is prohibiting you from plowing through every obstacle to help get your friends as close as possible to Jesus? You can do this! Be intentional in your prayer life, asking God to show you opportunities to engage your friends in some form of spiritual conversation.

RELENTLESS PURSUIT

In John 4, we find Jesus talking with a Samaritan woman. Verse 4 says, "Now [Jesus] had to go through Samaria." He could have been like every other Jew and walked around it. Remember, Jews didn't like going through Samaria. They didn't want anything to do with *those* people.

Yet, Jesus *had* to go there. He had a relentless passion to pursue all who were pushed to the fringes. So he came to a town in Samaria called Sychar. Jacob's well was there, and Jesus, tired from the journey, sat down by the well. It was about noon when a Samaritan woman came to draw water, and Jesus said to her, "Will you give me a drink?" (v. 7).

Jews and Samaritans didn't talk, and Jewish men definitely didn't talk to Samaritan women. But Jesus instinctively got curious about this woman. She mattered to Jesus and to God.

Jesus used his environment as an opportunity to talk about God's love. He talked about water, but he also talked about so much more. He talked about living water—that is, life in God—and he engaged with the woman's heart. He used water as an opportunity to draw out what she really thirsted for.

The woman shared a little bit of her story, and Jesus asked, "Why don't you get your husband, and we can drink together and talk?" When she told him she didn't have a husband, he replied, "The fact is, you have had five husbands, and the man you now have is not your husband" (v. 18).

"How did you even know this?" the woman said. "You must be a prophet."

Jesus hacked into this woman's story and shared with her about God. She realized that Jesus was something special and said, "I know that Messiah … is coming. When he comes, he will explain everything to us" (v. 25).

Then Jesus declared, "I, the one speaking to you—I am he" (v. 26). It was the first time Jesus trusted someone—a woman who had a scandalous past—with his full identity. Jesus constantly shattered stereotypes. He was always pushing boundaries, and he still pushes our boundaries—showing us how to love everyone, always.

The woman returned to her home and went throughout Samaria telling about her interaction with Jesus. The result: "Many of the Samaritans from that town believed in him because of the woman's testimony" (v. 39).

A life filled with scandal had been overwhelmed by grace. A holy urgency to spread this message empowered a dishonored woman to proclaim what Jesus had done. With unparalleled urgency, she challenged the community members to see for themselves. Many did, and what they found was a man who delivered hope, truth, and love like no other. As Jesus was leaving town, the people proclaimed, "We know that this man really is the Savior of the world" (v. 42).

It all began because Jesus just *had* to go to Samaria. Jesus showed up and began building a relationship with a Samaritan woman.

HEARING GOD'S WHISPERS

A few years ago, I traveled to the Middle East with a group of church leaders. One night in Bethlehem, I couldn't sleep. My hotel room didn't have Wi-Fi, but I thought I could access it free if I stood outside the shop next door. So I walked outside.

Unable to get a connection, I keep moving. There I was, at two o'clock in the morning, walking in the middle of the street, holding my phone up, staring at the bars, hoping for a connection. It was a beautiful night. I walked across the street and noticed a few people standing under a sign that read Hookah Lounge. As I got closer, I realized they were Palestinian soldiers with big guns.

Then I heard God whisper, *You should go talk with them.* My first response was, "And you should give me free Wi-Fi."

Again I heard God say, *I want you to go talk with them.*

Them? Those guys with the big guns? Are you kidding me? I felt tired and a little scared of these men. But I decided to go.

I walked toward them. I had absolutely no idea what to say. I mean, what's the best conversation starter in a situation like that? What do you say?

My palms were sweating, and I took a deep breath before saying, "It's really peaceful here in Bethlehem. Beautiful night. I'm Steve." I extended my arm and shook hands with the three guys. One of them looked at me and said, "Steve? Like the greatest US actor Steven Seagal?

"Yes!" I answered.

His eyes lit up. "Have you seen *Under Siege*?"

"Yeah." (Terrible movie, but I had seen it.)

So there I was, in the early morning hours, standing outside a hookah lounge, talking about terrible action movies with three Palestinian soldiers. As we talked, I had an internal conversation with God, asking the Spirit what to do next, because I was sure he wanted to do something in that moment.

Finally I asked the men, "Where do you live? You guys live here in Bethlehem?"

"No, we live in Nablus," one of them answered.

I said, "No way—Nablus? I'm going to be there on Thursday! We're going to a UN refugee camp called Balata."

That's where thirty thousand people live in two square miles. Dusty and loud, overcrowded and full of trash, this wasn't an easy place to live. In fact, it was horrible.

"That's where we live," said one soldier.

"Wow, we should meet in the courtyard," I told them. "I'll introduce you to my friends from California."

They said that would be great.

We met in Nablus on Thursday and had lunch together. It was all so surreal. A few nights earlier I was scared to talk with these three Palestinian soldiers, and now there they were laughing and connecting with our team.

After lunch we crossed the street from Balata, and a short walk from there was Jacob's well, where Jesus talked to the Samaritan woman. These guys were nonpracticing Muslims, so I asked if they knew what Jacob's well was. They said no, so I told them. "It's an ancient well that Jesus visited. The group I'm traveling with is going there now, and you've got to come and see it. You want to come with us?"

"Sure," one of them said. "We've never been in there before."

The place where Jacob's well is housed is now a church, and the well is below it. So we walked down a set of stairs to the well, which is still working and offers fresh water even today. With the group gathered around, I began to read aloud from John 4. I read about Jesus and the Samaritan woman. Then I started pulling up water in the well bucket. I asked, "What is it you thirst for? What is it you desire?"

Of course, my mind was spinning with what it must have been like for my new friends to be there. What were they thinking? Were they intrigued? Or was this not connecting at all? I knew they also spoke Arabic. In Arabic the word for "peace" is *salaam*. So I said, "How many of us desire peace and shalom and salaam?"

Those three guys raised their hands. I invited everyone to come up for a time of prayer and to taste some of the water. As people came forward, I sensed God whispering, *Go over to them.*

I walked up to the men, poured out some water, and said, "Do you desire living water? Do you desire to know Jesus? Do you desire true peace? Do you desire this?"

One by one they said yes—and they took the water and drank it.

At that moment I began to pray over them. It was holy ground, and we all felt it.

When the prayer ended, one of them took off his bracelet, a family heirloom, and put it around my wrist. He said, "Thank you. I will never be the same because of you. We didn't know this place existed. We never knew about Jesus."

If you think about it, this amazing experience started with a desire for connection. I was looking for an Internet connection, but God had a much better connection in mind. He simply whispered to me, *Go.* It all started with my willingness to respond: *I will go there. I will go to the other side. I will engage, and I will choose not to see guns or uniforms. I will choose not to see labels. I will choose not to see anything but what you desire, God.* I was willing to take a risk. Slowly but surely God gave me words. I began to strike up a friendship that led these Palestinian men to one of the most sacred places in the ancient Near East.

Would you go to the other side? Better said, what stops you from going to the other side? Fear? Feeling unprepared or unqualified? I felt all of those things that early morning in Bethlehem, and it breaks my heart when I think about how close I was to letting that keep me from participating in God's plan. Everyone is just a prayer and an invitation away. We're called to love everyone, always.

What are the faces and places you are praying for today? Are you drawing nearer to Jesus through the practices of reading his Word and having consistent prayer times? Are you listening for God's voice when you're out and about? Are you willing to set all fears aside and risk yourself to reach others? Humanity is thirsty for living water. We all desire connection, and the world desperately needs the peace that can come only from Jesus. When you're living this invitational life, you never know what will happen or how you'll impact eternity.

14
YOUR INVITATIONAL LIFE

Shortly after I got married, I began getting curious about my biological father, Chuck. Where did he live? What was he like? Did he ever think about me? Was he a follower of Jesus?

So I started conducting research and found out that Chuck lived in upstate New York. Filled with anticipation, my wife, Sarah, and I quickly booked plane tickets, hotel rooms, and a rental car.

I kept walking around our little apartment telling Sarah, "I can't believe we're actually going to meet Chuck!" All we had was his home address, so the plan was for me to just show up at the front door, ring the doorbell, and introduce myself. I realize now that this was probably not the best-thought-out plan.

As a boy I'd taken to thinking of Chuck as some kind of mythical creature. He was never around, my family rarely talked about him, and I began creating my own stories about the way I imagined him to be. When I was in seventh grade, I read Mitch Albom's book *Fab Five*. It details five freshman (Chris Webber, Jalen Rose, Juwan Howard, Jimmy King, and Ray Jackson) who went to the University of Michigan to play basketball. One chapter described how Jalen Rose's father saw him play basketball for the very first time.[1] His dad, Jimmy Walker, was a former NBA player who, after a basketball game, got a girl pregnant. Jimmy knew he had a son out there but had never met him. That is until one afternoon when he was working out at his local health club and watched his son on TV playing basketball for the University of Michigan.

Kids are very perceptive, but they're not always the best interpreters of reality. When I read that section about Jimmy Walker seeing his son play basketball for the first time, something within me clicked. I thought that if I played basketball in college, then Chuck would finally get to watch me. So each morning I woke up on a mission, looking to attack this dream so I could meet Chuck.

Fast-forward eight years, and I made the basketball team at California State University, Fullerton, as a walk-on. Leaving the gym one day, I suddenly realized that I was five foot eleven and weighed 175 pounds soaking wet. I didn't have a great jump shot. I had been dunked on more times than I had dunked. There was really no chance that Chuck would ever see me play basketball in college.

I walked back to my off-campus apartment weeping. The dream was over.

STUCK IN THE FAMILIAR

In the first chapter of Deuteronomy, we learn that for the past year, the Israelites had been camping out at Mount Horeb. During this time, they had become settled. They knew where they could get food and water, where to trade, and where to bring any disputes they had.

They had established a city that was safe and familiar. Without even knowing it, the Hebrew people had created a place where they were stuck. They didn't need to risk. They didn't need God. They had everything they needed.

God, however, had a bigger dream for the Hebrew people. It would require that they leave the familiar, risk it all, and depend on him. So God spoke up and said, "You have stayed long enough at this mountain" (1:6 NASB).

This Invitational Life is my attempt to redeem the least sexy word in all of Christendom: *evangelism*. It's a word that has been hijacked, misunderstood, and misused. In the wake of the breakdown, there are generations of people who have silenced their redemption stories. We have stayed long enough at this mountain.

Your entire life is about loving people well. Relationships that practice God's love with one another are the only thing you can bring with you into the next life. So you'll either risk all you have to align yourself with God's heartbeat for humanity or stay put, building a city miles away from the land of promise. It's your choice.

But before you choose, let's have an honest conversation about evangelism. What once meant "good news" now has been corrupted to be more about judging others than anything else. One of the primary ways evangelism is understood is in eschatological terms, which is just a fancy way of unpacking how things will end. When we understand evangelism in this way, it puts the emphasis on what happens when we die. It leads us to ask people we've never met before and with whom we have no relationship questions like, "If your life were to come to an end today, do you know where you would go?"

The foundation of eschatological evangelism looks like this:

- Sin
- Death
- Cross
- Fact
- Black and white
- Arrival in heaven
- Avoidance of the negative
- Dodging hell
- Fear
- Holy Bible

Good-hearted, well-intentioned Christ followers know that life on Earth is fleeting and fragile and will end. The urgent focus becomes helping people surrender their sins to the cross before that day comes. It's pretty black and white. You're either in or out. The motivation for introducing people to Jesus is to save them from an eternity spent burning in hell. This version of evangelism is entirely focused on "saving" as many souls as possible by creating a fear of hell and offering Jesus as the ticket out.

At best, this is the beginning step to growing into a relationship with Christ. At worst, it's simply fire insurance.

The problem is that people started going to low-income neighborhoods to evangelize by setting up a stage, playing a few worship songs, and sharing a message about sin, fire and brimstone, and the need for a savior. People would raise their hands, the pastor would say a dramatic prayer, and then the team would pack up, leaving these new followers of Jesus to figure things out on their own while the evangelists drove home fired up by their good work.

It isn't hard to see why this approach to evangelism would make some begin to feel burned out, since relationship wasn't part of the equation. Has there ever been a time when you've encountered this kind of outreach? Or perhaps at some point in your history, you've been the one pointing out someone's brokenness without consistently walking alongside as that person heals. What would it look like to do things differently now?

People began questioning whether this strategy of pushing into a community, announcing what was wrong, offering Jesus as the solution, and then packing up and leaving was actually helping. Sure, eternal salvation was crucial, but did that mean that life before death was meaningless? In this life, there were kids who needed mentors and parents who needed help developing job skills. There were disadvantages and a lack of consistent advocacy.

So the conversation of evangelism began to move from eschatology to ethics. A brand-new generation rose up determined to fix things. End poverty. End sex trafficking. End anything that was wrong, broken, or unjust. It was beautiful. Underneath this desire to evangelize through ethics was a plethora of presuppositions built upon

- Life
- Grace
- Resurrection
- Story
- Affirming the positive
- Living the kingdom of heaven
- Love
- The Holy Spirit

Good-hearted, well-intentioned Christ followers know that we'll all die and that we must work against any form of oppression or injustice that interrupts God's original good intent. The message of ethical evangelism is based primarily on love and grace. Those advocating this approach affirm the positive in others, telling them they were meant for so much more and inviting them to live out the kingdom of heaven empowered by the Holy Spirit.

One side is all about proclaiming. The other is all about demonstrating. The proclaimers focus primarily on *fall and redemption* while the demonstrators focus primarily on *creation and restoration.*

The proclaimers think the demonstrators who want to end the evils in this world are afraid to talk about sin. The demonstrators think the proclaimers who want to know where people will go when they die don't understand that we're called to live the gospel rather than just preach it.

So the proclaimers get louder.

And the demonstrators get quieter.

But the truth is, both are only half stories.[2]

We need a return to telling and living the *entire* story of ...

Creation.

Fall.

Struggle.

Redemption.

Restoration.

We need to find a better way to tell the whole story—a story that shows we're not afraid to talk about sin, the cross, grace, and resurrection. It's time to redeem the way we talk about the good news.

TURN, SET, GO

The Israelites were fixated on life around Mount Horeb. God wanted them to be a light to the nations, boldly showcasing his character to the rest of the world. However, that couldn't happen if they stayed stuck at the mountain. So he asked them to turn and face what he had for them: "You have stayed long enough at this mountain. Turn and set your journey, and go" (Deut. 1:6–7 NASB).

God gave the Hebrew people a vision of what he was hoping to do through them. This word *turn* conveys the same concept as the word *repentance*. To *repent* means "to turn your perspective, to change your philosophy and mind-set." It's a complete shift of your priorities to see a better way. God wants the entire nation to see the land of promise that is before them.

An invitational life—one that is open, rooted, accessible, and brave—is a beautiful life. It's a life filled with deep connection to the heart of God, a life that knows what love and grace feel like. It's a life that promises you a front-row seat to watch God at work in the people you're relating to. Life with God is your land of promise.

What do you need to walk away from that is keeping you from living a life like that? What keeps you from taking the risks to align yourself with God's heart? Is it fear of rejection? Fear of being misunderstood? Are you worried you won't do it right or maybe that you'll lose status? When was the last time you shared a meal with a nonbeliever? What was it like? Did you notice ways God was speaking to you during that time, revealing questions to ask and ways to listen? And if it's been a while since you've spent time with someone who is far from God, perhaps it's time to leave the mountain.

Perhaps its time to turn and see what God has put before you. Consider the faces and places you're feeling called to. What do you have to offer them? Your time? Your energy? Your story? Your insights, giftedness, and friendship? Turn and see that God wants to put your one and only life on display so that you might invite others into the greatest story ever told.

You're closer than you think to living this invitational life. It's in you. God hardwired you for this. His heart beats for people, and so can yours. What is so incredible is that God instructs his people to "turn and set your journey" (v. 7 NASB).

If you're ever going to get to the land of God's promise, you must set a plan. You must be intentional in your pursuit of this invitational life. It took the Hebrew people forty days to walk from the mountain to the Promised Land. What if we spent the next forty days focused on risking ourselves to align with God's heartbeat for humanity? How would we do that?

> 1. *Live*—Get swept up in God's great love and know your own relationship with God. This invitational life begins with your going deep with Jesus and then spills over to the rest of the world. Over the next forty days, read Scripture, walk through *This Invitational Life* study guide, and gather your small group to engage with the DVD as well.
>
> 2. *Show up*—Be expectant and available as you enter every place over the next forty days. The Holy Spirit wants to unleash you for kingdom good,

but you must be aware and open. Write down every prompting that comes from the Holy Spirit and decide right now that you will follow through quickly.

3. *Relate*—Over the next forty days, identify the people that God has put on your heart and relentlessly engage with them. Listen to them and relate to their stories. Become interesting to people by being interested in them. One of the easiest ways to go about this is by living this invitational life in community. Join a small group or gather with friends, and rally around these ideas for the next forty days to discover how God might use you.

4. *Risk*—Trust God by leaving the familiar and stepping into the unfamiliar; risk yourself to align with God's heartbeat for humanity. Make the difference you were created to make in the world. Over these next forty days, invite the people God has put on your heart to coffee, to church, to your house for a meal, or even to know Christ.

When you have a plan, your chances for success greatly increase. God told the Hebrew people to leave the mountain, turn, set the journey, and go. Once you know the plan, get after it. Go for it. Risk it all. Keep it at the forefront of your mind. I have this quote in my office: "Attack each day with an enthusiasm unknown to mankind." It serves as motivation to keep going. I want to risk my entire self with "an enthusiasm unknown to mankind" when God says, "Go!"

THE WORLD NEEDS RISK TAKERS

Earlier I left you hanging as Sarah and I were about ready to go meet Chuck. A few days before we were supposed to travel to New York to meet him, I received a call from the investigator who had helped us locate him. He had made a terrible mistake. Chuck had died a few years earlier of a massive heart attack. Talk about a kick to the gut. I didn't see that coming.

We had the entire trip booked, so we decided to stick with the plan and go anyway. When we arrived, we headed to the local cemetery to find Chuck's gravestone. I wanted a chance to say good-bye once and for all.

I began wandering around a massive courtyard dotted with tiny gray pieces of granite and cement, looking at the names in hopes of finding him. After a half hour of walking, I saw a tombstone that read "Charles Franklin Born." It was there, in the dewy grass under a huge oak tree, that I sat down to meet my biological father.

A few years ago I got an email from Chuck's widow. We had never met, but she reached out to say, "Steve, I came across one of your teachings. When I saw your picture and heard your voice, you looked and sounded just like your dad, and I had to get in touch with you."

So we started emailing back and forth, and I wrote, "I've just got a few questions to ask. One, how did Chuck die? Two, did he have any faith story at all? Three, did he ever think about me, ever talk about me? Four, what did he like to do?"

She wrote back and said, "He did think about you a lot. He actually had a baby picture of you on his mantle. Later in his life, someone shared the gospel with Chuck, and he came to faith."

At this moment, as I sat there taking in her words, my heart became so full of gratitude, it felt as if it might burst. I was and am so grateful for that person who shared his (or her) faith with Chuck. It was someone who realized that people far from God matter, and that person was willing to take a risk on a guy named Chuck.

The truth is, there are Chucks all around us. The Chucks of this world need us. The forgotten, forsaken places need us. But the question is, will we go? Will we leave the mountain? Will we redeem the word *evangelism*? Will we live, show up, relate, and risk it all? Will we live this invitational life? If we will, we might just change the life, and eternal life, of someone's father or mother or sibling or close friend.

BLESSING AND BENEDICTION

As long as I've been a teaching pastor, I've kept a tradition of benediction. A benediction is essentially a blessing spoken over another; it's a prayer of challenge, hope, and encouragement. At my home church of Willow Creek, we put our hands out and cup them as if we're catching water, and perhaps in a way we are.

Christ has given us the living water that leads to life with God. In this hope I offer the following blessing with open hands:

My brothers and sisters of this invitational life, may your funerals be packed with people who are nothing like you, because all were welcomed at your table. May you live a life deeply aligned with God's heartbeat for humanity, every single member of it. May you scatter seeds, looking for the good, looking for the need, relentlessly inviting others to come and see what God is doing in your life and the life of your church.

May you live the kind of wild and free Jesus life that forces people to say, "What happened here?" May you see your life as a carrier and not a barrier to helping people experience full access to God. May you remember that God's story is your story, and it's everyone's story. May you show up with great expectations, no matter where you are. Whether it's a prison or a coffee shop, may your story, all of it, be used to point people to the way of Jesus. May you listen to the whispers of the Spirit and chase after them quickly. May you incarnate the Lord's Prayer as the first disciples did in Acts 2. May you help others dominate life!

May God give you a new name as he did with Saul. May you outseek the seeker, keeping first things first, because in the end, it's simply Jesus plus nothing. May you dive in headfirst to help those you know who are drowning, willing to risk it all on the One who gave everything for you. May you risk even when it doesn't make sense. May you extend the invitation even to the people you can't stand, the people who are nothing like you, and may you have an urgency that rises up from within that makes you fill the seats in your car, tear out roofs, and approach soldiers on the other side of the world. May you go and live this invitational life!

ACKNOWLEDGMENTS

Thank you …

Sarah—this literally would not have been possible without you. It's an absolute privilege to walk through our one and only life together. WATW.

Emerson and **Mercy June**—it's an honor to be your dad. You teach me every day about joy and the goodness of God. Thank you. Love you.

Hidey Hole—each of you profoundly shaped me. It's a pleasure to have been able to grow up with you.

Wolfpack—life is always more fun with each of you. Let's keep taking pictures of the moon. See you in Shreveport.

Rob and **Kristen**—thank you for the invitation to come change the world one west Michigan at a time.

Mike and **Justina**—study the Scriptures, a little omelet parlor (moment of silence), message prep, and some afternoon hoops made up one of my favorite seasons of life.

Hal and **Chrissie**—thank you. No words can accurately describe what Hal meant to me. I miss him so much.

Bill and **Lynne**—thank you for inviting me to join Willow Creek, for teaching me about the church, leadership, teaching, and peacemaking.

Dominate—I wouldn't be here without your example.

MHS—whether it was serving in the element, foursquare with students from anthem or fifty-6, or hanging with some of the most incredible volunteers on the planet … thank you.

RHF—I'll never forget 2/28/10 and what began. You showed me what was possible, and I'll never forget the gift of serving with each of you.

Solidarity—you never cease to inspire me. So proud of each of you and what I've learned about the way of Jesus through you.

Willow Creek—it's such an honor to serve you. Your heart for the Scriptures and the world, and your incredible generosity remind me each weekend about the power and beauty of the local church.

Salvation Army—thanks for inviting me into the family. You continue to inspire me, and I love how much God is teaching me through you.

JJ—thanks for drawing this book out and making me believe the dream was possible.

Tim—thanks for pushing this book forward. Thanks for believing in my vision.

Alice and Ingrid—thanks for your patience, kindness, and help to make this project all it could be.

Aaron—I appreciate you more than you'll ever know.

Andrew—love our weekly chats. Thanks for being in it with me.

Blaine—thanks for sharing your creativity with me; you inspire me. And thanks for showing up on Thursday mornings.

Shauna—thanks for coaching me through all of this. Sorry for blowing up your phone with questions, but you have been such a help.

Tim Schraeder—I think we could change the world.

Avengers—that's for you, Colby! Let's keep doing this!

Penhales—thanks for introducing me to the army. You are two of my favorite people on the planet.

Ed Laity—thanks for your constant encouragement. The world would be a better place if everyone had someone like you in their life.

Dad—this has been my favorite season. Grateful for El Cajete and time with you.

Mike and **Jen**—thank you for welcoming me fully and showing me what love looks like. Cannot imagine my life without you two.

Jim Harbaugh—thanks for coming back to Ann Arbor. Hail to the Victors.

There is so much more I want to write because so many of you played a key role in making this possible. Promisetown. Tranquil Tea. Lucky Monk. JVR. TIL street team. TIL album musicians. Willow staff (wish I could thank each of you). Camarillo. David C Cook for believing in this. Hume Lake. CIY. Todd Proctor for teaching me about the HS. Haliburtons. Hugheses and Bacons. Dick Robinson. Ken Lee. Allees. Gibbo. Deegans. Telos, for teaching me about the power of beatitudes and peace. Dakota, for helping with all the details. Netty, for all your wisdom and heart and great taste in music. Margaret Hogan, for being the funniest. The Benoits, for moving east. Thank you, friends.

NOTES

#WELCOME

1. Estimate from United Nations Department of Economic and Social Affairs, Population Division, cited in "World Population Clock," Worldometers, accessed March 14, 2016, www.worldometers.info/world-population/.

2. "Host Michigan Bests Notre Dame before Record Crowd of 115,109," ESPN, September 8, 2013,http://espn.go.com/college-football/recap?gameId =332500130.

3. "QuickFacts: Ann Arbor, Michigan," US Census Bureau, accessed March 14, 2016, www.census.gov/quickfacts/table/PST045215/2603000.

4. Centers for Disease Control and Prevention, "Current Depression among Adults—United States, 2006 and 2008," *Morbidity and Mortality Weekly Report* 59, no. 38 (October 1, 2010): 1229–35; see also Ray Hainer, "CDC: Nearly 1 in 10 U.S. Adults Depressed," *Health*, September 30, 2010, http://news.health.com/2010/09/30/cdc-depression-survey/.

5. Survey data cited in Janice Shaw Crouse, "The Loneliness of American Society," *American Spectator*, May 18, 2014, http://spectator.org/articles/59230 /loneliness-american-society.

6. Aaron Niequist, "Changed," *With Broken Fists* © 2008 AaronNieq Music.

CHAPTER 1—MY STORY, OUR STORY

1. N. T. Wright, *The Last Word: Scripture and the Authority of God* (New York: HarperCollins, 2006). The author uses a five-act structure—Creation, Fall, Israel, Jesus, and the Church—that greatly helped me with this chapter.

CHAPTER 2—FROM SIMPLE TO SACRED

1. "Apple Presents iPod," Apple Press Info, October 23, 2001, www.apple.com/pr
   /library/2001/10/23Apple-Presents-iPod.html.

CHAPTER 3—BARRIERS OR CARRIERS

1. United Nations, "Outreach Programme on the Rwanda Genocide and the
   United Nations," accessed March 18, 2016, www.un.org/en/preventgenocide
   /rwanda/education/rwandagenocide.shtml; "Statistics," SURF Survivors Fund,
   accessed March 18, 2016, http://survivors-fund.org.uk/resources/rwandan
   -history/statistics/.

2. United Nations High Commission for Refugees, *World at War: UNHRC Global
   Trends Forced Displacement in 2014* (Geneva: UNHRC, 2015), 2.

CHAPTER 4—BONE MARROW

1. Mike Erre, one of my favorite teachers, greatly influenced this section. We used
   to meet for breakfast weekly, and one morning we spent a portion talking
   about Ephesus. It opened my eyes to see that city and my own story in completely new ways.

CHAPTER 6—*MASSEVOT*

1. In the early 2000s, I had the chance to meet with Ray Vander Laan for breakfast
   at a truck stop outside Holland, Michigan. It was like drinking from a fire
   hydrant. He taught me all about the concept of *massevot.*

2. Austin Gutwein, interview by Ashley Judd, CBS *Final Four Show*, April 5, 2008,
   www.cbspressexpress.com/cbs-sports/releases/view?id=18289; www.youtube
   .com/watch?v=d_754g-beMQ.

3. A friend of mine, Doug Bacon, taught me this simple prayer over lunch one
   day. I've carried it with me ever since that epic Wahoo's meal.

CHAPTER 7—DELIBERATELY INTENTIONAL

1. Cited in Glenn Llopis, "6 Ways Effective Listening Can Make You a Better
   Leader," *Forbes*, May 20, 2013, www.forbes.com/sites/glennllopis
   /2013/05/20/6-effective-ways-listening-can-make-you-a-better-leader
   /#729dfe8bbf6c.

2. Llopis, "6 Ways."

CHAPTER 8—DOMINATE

1. Definition from Jon Morrissette, Lakeside Christian Church, Springfield, Illinois.

CHAPTER 9—CURIOUS

1. Stephanie Carlson, cited in Susan Robertson, "Why You Should Have a Child-Like Imagination (and the Research That Proves It)," *Ideas to Go*, March 2013, www.ideastogo.com/the-science-of-imagination.

2. Film transcript, Sir Ken Robinson, *Do Schools Kill Creativity?*, TED.com, February 2006, www.ted.com/talks/ken_robinson_says_schools_kill_creativity/transcript?language=en.

CHAPTER 11—"HELP!"

1. Lawrence Kushner, in "The World Is Full of God," *U.S. Catholic*, July 25, 2008, www.uscatholic.org/life/2008/07/the-world-full-god.

CHAPTER 14—YOUR INVITATIONAL LIFE

1. Mitch Albom, *Fab Five* (New York: Warner Books, 1993), 169–70.

2. Gabe Lyons, *The Next Christians: How a New Generation Is Restoring the Faith* (New York: Doubleday, 2010), 51–54.